ASSHUR the ASSYRIAN

T0208421

ASSHUR the ASSYRIAN

by
Allen Bonck

iUniverse, Inc.
New York   Bloomington

ASSHUR the ASSYRIAN

iUniverse books may be ordered through booksellers or by contacting:

iUniverse
1663 Liberty Drive
Bloomington, IN 47403
www.iuniverse.com
1-800-Authors (1-800-288-4677)

Because of the dynamic nature of the Internet, any Web addresses or links contained in this book may have changed since publication and may no longer be valid. The views expressed in this work are solely those of the author and do not necessarily reflect the views of the publisher, and the publisher hereby disclaims any responsibility for them.

ISBN: 978-1-4401-6273-2 (pbk)
ISBN: 978-1-4401-6275-6 (hc)
ISBN: 978-1-4401-6274-9 (ebk)

Bible references are from the King James Bible
Bold text, underlines and emphasis added.
Book graphics are by the author.

Printed in the United States of America

iUniverse rev. date: 10/13/2009

"Insignia of Sargon - used by modern Assyrians atop their new flag."

DEDICATION

To Pastor Robert Hooley, who in 1974 wrote the booklet *ANTICHRIST,* which provided me with the foundation of scriptural understanding to study Asshur the Assyrian.

SYMBOL GLOSSARY

A glossary of the symbols used at the start of each chapter.

Introduction: The flag used by modern Assyrians to represent the revived nation of Assyria. Note that the symbol of the god Asshur found in the upper center of the flag is shown in the war position.

Chapter One: The symbol represents the old Assyrian god Asshur in the peace position. The bow is lowered, his hand is outstretched, and he is facing to his right. Asshur, the man, starts his rule as a man of peace.

Chapter Two: The two flags are the new Assyrian flag and the Iranian flag. It is meant to represent the connection between the two nations relating to Asshur the Persian.

Chapter Three: The symbol is meant to represent the Prophet Daniel's vision of the Fourth Beast, as found in Daniel 7. The ten ho•rns represent the ten kings of the final kingdom of this world. The small horn is eleventh, and is Asshur the little horn.

Chapter Four: The symbol represents the ten horns and ten kings of the Beasts kingdom. The 666 is the number of his name, used to identify his followers.

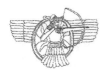

Chapter Five: The symbol represents the god Asshur, shown in the war position. He is poised to strike with his bow drawn and aimed. Asshur is now facing to his left. This indicates that Asshur, the man, will turn from a man of peace to a man of war and will break his treaties.

Chapter Six: The symbol is an ancient Assyrian dagger. It represents the weapon used by a man in Asshur's stronghold to assassinate him.

CONTENTS

A DESCRIPTIVE OUTLINE

General:

This book is a biblical exposition of the man called Asshur the Assyrian. There are many books that explore the history of Assyria and the many kings who ruled there. This book explores the history of Assyria only briefly but covers the future nation and the man who will lead her. The revived nation of Assyria will play more than a small part in the prophetic events coming in the near future. Assyria's leader will rule much more than just a small province in northern Iraq. He will ultimately rule the world.

Chapters:

Chapter One: "Asshur the Assyrian" (pages 5–28) establishes the existence of an Assyrian nation and leader in the last days, which is the time of the return of the Messiah to deliver Israel and set up the Messianic kingdom. The following prophetic biblical chapters are studied: Micah 5; Isaiah: 10, 14, 23, 30, 31

Chapter Two: "Asshur and Persia" (pages 29-40) explores the Persian connection with the Assyrian leader. Asshur the Assyrian is ethnically an Assyrian but is also an Iranian citizen and political leader. He will eventually rule Iran.

This chapter also explores the Armageddon sequence of battles and Asshur's influence and participation. The following prophetic biblical chapters are studied: Daniel 10–11.

Chapter Three: "Asshur and the Little Horn" (pages 41-50) explains the symbolism used in the book of Daniel to reveal the final king and kingdom that will exist just prior to the establishment of God's kingdom on earth. Daniel's little horn is identified and his association with the final ten-nation kingdom is exposed. The following prophetic biblical chapters are studied: Daniel 7–8.

Chapter Four: "Asshur the Beast" (pages 51-66) ties the symbolism of the Book of Revelations to Daniel's beasts and to Asshur. Tremendous insights into Assyria and Asshur are found in Revelations that are not found anywhere else in scripture. The following prophetic biblical chapters are studied in this chapter: Daniel 2; Joel 2; I John 2; Revelation 13, 15, 16, 17, 19, 20.

Chapter Five: "Asshur the Son of Perdition" (pages 67-72) reveals Asshur by several additional names and further defines the man and his activities. Asshur is called the "son of perdition," "Man of sin" and "that Wicked." The following prophetic biblical chapters are studied in this chapter: II Thessalonians 2; John 14; I John 2.

Chapter Six: "Asshur, One Man's Story" (pages 73-88) paints a picture of Asshur's life from all the scriptures and cultural information available at this time. Asshur was given a call (charge) by God to do certain tasks for God but drifts away in his heart. Asshur accomplishes things in his life that no other man has ever done.

Maps:

Indexes and Summaries: This book includes informational summaries within the chapters to aid the reader in studying and referencing information and scriptures. The following indexes are provided at back of the book:

INTRODUCTION

Asshur and Assyria

The name Asshur is first found in scripture in the book of Genesis 10:11 and 22. Asshur is identified as the grandson of Noah and the son of Shem. He was also the brother of Arphaxad, who was the father of the lineage of the Hebrews, those who would become known as Jews.

Asshur is also credited with the founding of the cities of Nineveh, Rehoboth, and Calah. Nineveh became the capitol of the nation that would bear Asshur's name: Assyria. The scriptural word for Asshur is used for the man, his descendants, and also the land of Assyria, which is located in the northern part of modern Iraq. This land is also known as northern Mesopotamia, the land between the rivers, or the plains of Shinar. Ancient Mesopotamia consisted of three major nations—in the south was Chaldea, in the central plain was Babylon, and to the north was Assyria.

At some point in time, the chief deity of Assyria was also called Asshur. Asshur the god was probably the equivalent to the Babylonian god Bel, the Canaanite Baal, and the Egyptian Osiris. These deities were not sun gods but were the "sun-like" gods, and their appearance shined like the sun. The Babylonian Bel can be identified as the scriptural Lucifer found in Isaiah 14:12.

The early Assyrian kings are known as the kings who lived in tents. These kings reigned from about 3000 to 2400 BC. The Assyrians did not become an empire until about 2400 BC when Sargon I came to power. The Assyrians were at times totally independent and at other times they were dominated by other Mesopotamian nations: the Akkadians, Sumerians, or Babylonians. The late period of Assyrian kings runs from 911 BC to 612 BC and ends with the sacking of Nineveh by the Medes.

This is considered the end of the Assyrian Empire however, the nation and people continued to exist.

According to modern Assyrian tradition, the king of Assyria in AD 33 converted to Christianity, and the entire nation soon followed. The national conversion took place during the first century AD, and even today, some estimates have as many as 94 percent of modern Assyrians to be Christian. The modern Assyrian Christians belong basically to four churches, which came from the same ancient church. They are the Chaldean, Syriac Orthodox, Church of the East, and the Syriac Catholic (the term catholic means "universal," not a specific connection the Roman Catholic Church). There are some more recent Assyrian churches that have sprung from twentieth-century British influence and are based on the Protestant Reformation. They include the Assyrian Evangelical Church and the Assyrian Pentecostal Church.

Early in the twentieth century, the Assyrian people to a large extent fled their land and went into Diaspora around the world. This is due largely to suffering and persecution at the hands of the adherents of Islam. It's hard to know just how many Assyrians there are today—most estimates seem to agree to about 3.3 million worldwide. There could be as few as 500,000 living in Iraq today. Most would be in the homeland area of northern Iraq known today as the "Nineveh Plains" (see map-3, p.91).

The year 2008 was a hard year for Assyrians in Iraq; many have fled to Syria and Jordan to escape persecution from militant Islam. The recent American military intervention in Iraq and removal of Saddam Hussein and his government has created a completely new dynamic in the area and may ultimately lead to favorable conditions for the Assyrian people to return to their homeland.

There has developed, starting in the mid to late twentieth century, a movement to reestablish an independent Assyrian nation in the homeland of northern Iraq. It appears that progress has been made and many world leaders are now aware of the need for the Assyrian nation. There are scriptures indicating that there will be an Assyrian nation in the last days and into the millennium. The most well known reference is in Isaiah 19:23–25.

> (23) In that day shall there be a highway out of Egypt to Assyria, and the Assyrian shall come into Egypt and the Egyptian into

Assyria, and the Egyptians shall serve with the Assyrians. (24) In that day shall Israel be the third with Egypt and with Assyria, even a blessing in the midst of the land: (25) Whom the LORD of hosts shall bless, saying, Blessed be Egypt my people, and Assyria the work of my hands, and Israel mine inheritance.

This situation has never existed in history and will be set in the time just after the great tribulation, the time when God deals with the sins of the nations and sets up the Messianic Kingdom, Christ's thousand-year millennial reign.

The nation of Iraq, which we know today was the creation of the British and will not be intact at the end of the age but will most likely be called Assyria.

CHAPTER ONE

Asshur
the Assyrian

In the introduction, you learned of the original man called Asshur and how from him came the nation and empire of Assyria. Also, I discussed how Assyria is currently in Diaspora but with hopes and aspirations to be a nation once again.

This chapter will cover a man called Asshur "The Assyrian," who will be a modern man and part of the Assyrian restoration. God, through the Hebrew prophets, has much to say about this man. We will study Micah 5: and five chapters from Isaiah. Each chapter we study will add some information and understanding about Asshur. I will show that these prophecies were written for the last days and are yet to be fulfilled. We will start with a study of Micah 5:

> (1) Now gather thyself in troops, O daughter of troops: <u>he</u> [the Assyrian] hath laid siege against <u>us</u> [Israel]; they shall smite the judge of Israel with a rod upon the cheek. (2) But thou, Bethlehem Ephratah, though thou be little among the thousands of Judah, yet out of thee shall he come forth unto me that is to be ruler in Israel; whose goings forth have been from old, from everlasting. [The Messiah] (3) Therefore will he give them up, until the time that she which travaileth hath brought forth: then the remnant of his brethren shall return unto the children of Israel. (4) And he shall stand and feed in the strength of the LORD, in the majesty of the name of the LORD his God; and they shall abide: for now shall he be great unto the ends of the earth. (5) And this man [the Messiah]

shall be the peace, when **the Assyrian** shall come into **our land** [Israel]: and when he shall tread in our palaces, then shall we raise against him seven shepherds and eight principal men. (6) And they shall waste the **land of Assyria** with the sword, and the **land of Nimrod** in the entrances thereof: thus shall he [the Messiah] deliver us from **the Assyrian**, when **he** cometh into our land [Israel], and when he treadeth within our borders.

Assyrians have come into Israel many times through out history, but this event will happen at the time that the Messiah, the man from Bethlehem, comes to rule in Israel. He will be there to set up his kingdom. Jews are awaiting the Messiah, and the Christians are looking for his return. In either case, it has not yet happened. Historically, Israel has never attacked the land of Assyria as described in verse 6. This means that this man called the Assyrian and the land (nation) of Assyria are still to come. At the time this prophecy is fulfilled, there will be a nation of Israel and also a nation of Assyria.

(7) And **the remnant of Jacob [Israel] shall be in the midst of many people** as a dew from the LORD, as the showers upon the grass, that tarrieth not for man, nor waiteth for the sons of men. (8) And **the remnant of Jacob shall be among the Gentiles in the midst of many people** as a lion among the beasts of the forest, as a young lion among the flocks of sheep: who, if he go through, both treadeth down, and teareth in pieces, and none can deliver. (9) Thine hand shall be lifted up upon thine adversaries; and all thine enemies shall be cut off.

These scriptures speak to the Jewish Diaspora, which has put Jews among the gentiles since about AD 70. We saw the establishment of the nation of Israel in 1948 and the return of many Jews to their home. They have not yet seen all their enemies cut off, because the Messiah has not come for that purpose and the Assyrian is not yet king in Assyria. It says in verse 3 that he (the Messiah) will give them up until she comes forth from her travail. It's clear today that Israel is in travail from the nations all around her; she is under constant threat of attack and destruction. Even Europe has manifest anti-Semitism.

(10) And it shall come to pass **in that day**, saith the LORD, that I will cut off thy horses out of the midst of thee, and I will destroy thy chariots: (11) And I will cut off the cities of thy land [Israel], and throw down all thy strong holds: (12) And I will cut off witchcrafts out of thine hand; and thou shalt have no more soothsayers: (13) Thy graven images also will I cut off, and thy standing images out of the midst of thee; and thou shalt no more worship the work of thy hands. (14) And I will pluck up thy groves out of the midst of thee: **so I will destroy thy cities. (15) And I will execute vengeance in anger and fury upon the heathen, such as they have not heard**.

It's not always easy to see God's purpose in prophetic events. God clearly will deliver Israel from their enemies, and yet, at same time deal with Israel's sins. He will not allow Israel to enter into the millennium—his rest—carrying their sin. The works of their hands and their weapons of war will be taken away. Nothing will remain that can get between God and his people. This is also true of all the nations of the world not, just Israel. Assyria will be broken before becoming the "work of my hands" (Isaiah 19:25). Also God will deal with the gentile nations, as explained in verse 15 above.

The events detailed in this prophecy will take place in the time of God's wrath, a time when the world's sin and pride will exceed God's threshold of tolerance. And God will move to judge the nations in his wrath and anger. The Assyrian's military attack and occupation of Israel is also seen in Jesus's warnings about the "end."

Luke 21:20–22: And **when ye shall see Jerusalem compassed with armies,** then know that the desolation thereof is nigh. (21) Then let them which are in Judaea **flee to the mountains**; and let them which are in the midst of it [Judea/Israel] depart out; and let not them that are in the countries enter thereinto. (22) For these are **the days of vengeance**, that all things which are written may be fulfilled.

In Matthew 24 the inhabitants of Judaea are told to flee to the mountains when they see the abomination of desolation stand in the holy place.

Matthew 24:15 and 16: When ye therefore shall see **the abomination of desolation,** spoken of by Daniel the prophet, stand in the holy place, (whoso readeth, let him understand:) (16) Then let them which be in Judaea **flee into the mountains**:

The Assyrian is the king who commands the armies which come into Israel at the time of the end and the days of vengeance and is dealt with by Christ (this man will be the peace when the Assyrian cometh into our land. Micah 5:5). The Assyrian is also the man who sets up the abomination of desolation in the holy place, the Jewish temple in Jerusalem. It will become clear further in this scripture study what the abomination actually is.

Descriptive Summary of Micah 5

1. The fulfillment of Micah's prophecy is set for the end times, a time when the Jewish messiah delivers Israel and the Jewish people from an attack from a man called Asshur the Assyrian when he treadeth within our borders. Verses 2–5

2. There will be an end-time restored nation of Israel and also a nation of Assyria. Verses 3 and 6

3. It will be a time when the Jewish people are both in the Land of Israel and in Diaspora among the gentiles. Verses 7 and 8

4. It is the time that the Lord deals (judges) with Israel's sin. He destroys the works of their hands. Verses 10–14

5. With the Messiah's help Israel attacks and wastes the land of Assyria. Verses 5 and 6

Isaiah 10

"The Rod of my Anger"
(1) Woe unto them that decree unrighteous decrees, and that write grievousness which they have prescribed; (2) To turn aside

the needy from judgment, and to take away the right from the poor of my people, that widows may be their prey, and that they may rob the fatherless!

These verses explain why Israel will be judged and specifically what their sins are. The lawmakers, those who make decrees (laws) are not protecting the poor, widows, and fatherless. Their priorities are toward those who have clout, not the vulnerable of society. It's clear that while legislators have authority in this world and its governments to make laws and set values, they will be held accountable to God and his values in the end.

> (3) And what will ye do in the **day of visitation** [accountability], and in the desolation which shall come from afar? to whom will ye flee for help? and where will you leave your glory? (4) Without me [the LORD] they shall bow down under the prisoners, and they shall fall under the slain. For all this his [the LORD'S] **anger is not turned away**, but his hand is stretched out still.

This will be the time of visitation and desolation. Israel's leaders will have no place to turn, and they will be prisoners and will be slain for their sin.

> (5) **O Assyrian**, the rod of mine anger [the LORD'S], and the staff in their [the Assyrians] hand is mine [the LORD'S] indignation. (6) I [the LORD] will send him [the Assyrian] against an hypocritical nation [Israel], and against the people of my wrath will **I give him a charge** [an order], to take the spoil, and to take the prey, and to tread them down like the mire of the streets.

It is clear from these two verses that the Lord is behind Israel's judgment and that the Assyrians (the army) and the Assyrian (the man) are being used by God to be his rod. The discipline is from God, and the tool is Assyria.

(7) Howbeit he [the Assyrian] meaneth not so, neither doth his heart think so; but it is **in his heart to destroy and cut off nations not a few** (8) For he saith, Are not my princes altogether kings? (9) Is not Calno as Carchemish? is not Hamath as Arpad? Is not Samaria as Damascus? (10) As my hand hath found the kingdoms of the idols, and whose graven images did excel them of Jerusalem and of Samaria; (11) Shall I not, as I have done unto Samaria and her idols, so do to Jerusalem and her idols? (12) Wherefore **it shall come to pass, that when the Lord hath performed his whole work upon mount Zion and on Jerusalem, I [the Lord] will punish the fruit of the stout heart of the king of Assyria**, and the glory of his **high looks**, (13) for he saith. By the strength of <u>my hand</u> I have done it, and by **my wisdom**; for **I am prudent**: and I have removed the bounds of the people, and have robbed their treasures, and I have put down the inhabitants like a **valiant man**: (14) And **my hand** hath found as a nest the riches of the people: and as one gathereth eggs that are left, have **I have gathered all the earth**; and there was **none that moved the wing, or opened the mouth, or peeped**.

Asshur has his own agenda beyond what the Lord wants done. His scope of control is "nations not a few." In fact he will control the entire world for a short time: "I have gathered all the earth." Asshur will become so powerful and subdue the nations so completely that no one will dare say anything against him: "there was none that moved the wing, or opened the mouth, or peeped."

Asshur also makes a case to justify his pride and arrogance by showing how great his princes are and how easily he has destroyed nations and taken all their riches. He is able to destroy their governments and take away their control: "I have removed the bounds of the people." He then takes full credit for all the success Assyria has had: "My hand" "My wisdom" "I am prudent" "a valiant man." He has certainly done something that no one else has ever done. He has conquered the whole earth. No king or emperor in all of history has ever accomplished this feat.

It comes with one big problem: He has defied God, and he is boasting against the Lord. But the Lord is not afraid to peep. And when God decides to speak, the earth will shake. The Lord states that when he is through dealing with Israel (Zion) and when his complete work is done, he will punish Asshur.

> (15) Shall the axe boast itself against him that heweth therewith? Or shall the saw magnify itself against him that shaketh it? As if the rod should shake itself against them that lift it up, or as the staff should lift up itself, as if it were no wood.

Clearly, the Assyrian is the rod, which God uses to judge nations, nothing more! The Lord allows the Assyrian to succeed until the time comes to punish him. The Assyrian nation and their allies will not escape God's dealing.

> (16) Therefore shall the Lord, the Lord of hosts, send among his [the Assyrian's] fat ones leanness; and under his glory he [the Lord] shall kindle a burning like the burning of a fire. (17) And the **light of Israel** shall be for a fire, and **his Holy One** [Messiah] for a flame: and it shall burn and devour his thorns and his briers in one day; (18) And shall consume the glory of his forest, and his fruitful field, **both soul and body**: and they shall be as when the standard bearer fainteth. (19) And the rest of the trees of the forest shall be few, that a child may write them.

God's judgment comes upon Asshur's "fat ones." It's obvious that Asshur is not the only one who is lifted up in pride. Asshur deliberately instilled a sense of uniqueness in his followers so they would feel special and thus not have pity or feel sorry for their victims. Asshur's Army(s) is referred to as thorns and briers and they are burned in battle with the Holy One of God (the light of Israel). This is reference to the Messiah who will come to deliver Israel—the same man as found in Micah 5:2.

The battle results in more than just the physical death of the soldiers on the field but also the judgment of the soul after death. "both soul and body" they shall be consumed by fire.

> (20) And it shall come to pass **in that day**, **that the remnant of Israel**, and such as are escaped of the house of Jacob, shall no

more again **stay** on **him that smote them**; but shall **stay** upon the LORD, the Holy One of Israel in truth. (21) The remnant shall return, even the remnant of Jacob, unto the mighty God. (22) For though thy people **Israel be as the sand of the sea**, **yet a remnant of them shall return**: the **consumption** decreed shall overflow with righteousness. (23) for the Lord GOD of hosts shall make a **consumption**, even determined, in the midst of the land.

The reference in verse 20 to "such as are escaped" speaks to those in Judea (house of Jacob) who will flee to the mountains when they see Jerusalem encompassed about with armies (Luke 21:20–22). There will be a remnant of Jews escaping from the Assyrian and hiding in the wilderness till the consumption is past.

The term "stay" as used in verse 20 means to trust. Israel put their trust in the Assyrian. It's not clear in this chapter why they trusted him or what kind of agreement they had with him, only that they will never again trust in man for their security and peace but will trust in the Lord for their needs. This change in attitude is a part of the whole work that the Lord will do in Zion. It's tempting for us to question or judge Israel for leaning on the Assyrian. But we all tend to trust that which we can see and touch. The Assyrian is a flesh and blood man with whom they can negotiate and sign a paper. This is much easier than walking by faith in an invisible God.

There is in Isaiah 28 a prophecy to the Jewish rulers in Jerusalem set at the time of the end of the age—a time the Lord is a diadem to his people. This prophecy refers to a covenant that Israel has made with death and hell.

Isaiah 28: (15) Because ye have said, We have made **a covenant with death and with hell** are we at agreement: when the overflowing scourge shall pass through, it shall not come unto us: for we have made lies our refuge [stay], and under falsehood have we hid ourselves; (18) And **your covenant with death shall be disannulled**, and your agreement with hell shall not stand; when the overflowing scourge shall pass through, then **ye shall be trodden down by it**.

The armies spoken of in Luke 21, which attack Judea and Jerusalem and which are lead by Asshur are this overflowing scourge. The covenant will be annulled and Israel will be trodden down till the Israeli's are delivered by the Holy One of Israel, the man from Bethlehem.

The consumption spoken of in verses 22 and 23 is the scourge that will pass through the land of Israel to judge it. Although God allows the consumption, it won't totally destroy Israel. It won't kill all his people; he saves a remnant.

The Lord wants his people to understand what is happening to them and to be encouraged to persevere through the time of his anger. He tells his people not to be afraid of the Assyrian and that the indignation will last only a very little while. We know that many will be killed during this time. The Lord must be encouraging his people, those who flee to the mountains, those who in obedience have responded to his exhortation to flee.

> (24) Therefore thus saith the Lord GOD of hosts, O **my people that dwellest in Zion**, be not afraid of **the Assyrian**: **he shall smite thee with a rod**, and shall lift up his staff against thee, after the manner of Egypt. (25) For **yet a very little while, and the indignation shall cease**, and mine anger in their destruction. (26) And the LORD of hosts shall stir up a scourge for him [the Assyrian] according to the slaughter of Midian at the rock Oreb: and as his rod was upon the sea, so shall he lift it up after the manner of Egypt. (27) And **it shall come to pass in that day, that his burden shall be taken away from off thy shoulder, and his yoke from off thy neck**, and the yoke **shall be destroyed because of the anointing**.

The anointing is God's presence. He will always be close to his people and his anointed one, the Messiah will deal with the Assyrian. His yoke will be removed and the burden lifted. The Lord tells his people in Matthew 11:29 and 30:

> Take my yoke upon you, and learn of me; for I am meek and lowly in heart: and ye shall find rest unto your souls. (30) For my yoke is easy and my burden is light.

The final verses in Isaiah 10 present the literal movements of Asshur as he proceeds through the land on his way to Jerusalem. Based on this account, the inhabitants of Jerusalem would have time, if they move quickly, to escape the city.

The names of the locations mentioned in this account can be found in other locations in scripture. Most of them are in I Samuel. Scholars have been able to locate all but a few of these towns and to map them (see map-4, p.92). I have taken these locations and overlaid them on a current map of the area to better understand the path the Assyrian will take. The first location mentioned is Aiath, which has also been called Ai. There is no modern town or village at that location, but there is an historic site that is known today as "the village of Asur" and also "the village of Baal." Hazar Baal marks the location.

It is amazing that the biblical account about the movements of the Assyrian, starts at a village in Judea that is called Tall Assur, which is a simple spelling for Asshur or Assyrian. It says he has come to Aiath and then passes on to Migron, which is approximately four miles southeast and continues to Michmash a few miles beyond but still in the valley. In Michmash, he "hath laid up his carriages." The Hebrew words indicate that he is mustering his wheeled weapons at this location. There is still a village at this location called Mikhmas and there appears to be room to assemble a lot of equipment there. Modern Mikhmas is a short distance off the main road.

The armies continue from Mikhmas up the hills to over the pass (passage) to the village of Geba that is on top of the ridge. Asshur has now traveled up from the great rift, which runs the length of Israel from the valley below Jerusalem. It says that they lodge at Geba, modern Jaba, at least one night, maybe more. It's clear that Asshur has a large army or armies. They can get strung out very easily, They also don't stop easily, and they don't start easily.

At this time, the neighboring towns are in a panic. It states that Ramah, modern Ramallah, is afraid. They are only two miles west of his position. Gibeah is fled; the inhabitants have evacuated, and they are only three miles to the southwest of Jaba and nearly in line of Asshur's path. Gillim is told to lift up thy voice; this is to sound an alarm. Gillim is directly in Asshur's path. Anathoth, is called "O poor Anathoth" because it is in the way.

If the modern location of Anata is Anathoth, then the Assyrians will probably split and come to Jerusalem on two different roads (see map-4, p.92). Madmenah is removed—the Hebrew for removed means "they flee and evacuate"—and the villagers of Gebim will gather themselves to flee. Asshur comes to the location of Nob, and he remains at that location all day. Nob was located just north of Jerusalem and the Temple Mount. Asshur's armies would have just moved into the area from the modern Atarot industrial zone. The term "remains" means he stops and stands up; he prepares to strike.

Asshur shakes his hand against Jerusalem and the Temple Mount, the hill of Jerusalem, Mount Zion. We will find through additional scripture studies in the books of Daniel and Revelations that the occupation of Jerusalem will last for three and one half years.

> (28) He is come to **Aiath**, he is passed to **Migron**; at **Michmash** he hath laid up his carriages: (29) They are gone over the passage: they have taken up their lodging at **Geba**; **Ramah** is afraid; **Gibeah** of Saul is fled. (30) Lift up thy voice, O daughter of **Gallim**: cause it to be heard unto Laish, O poor **Anathoth**. (31) **Madmenah** is removed; the inhabitants of **Gebim** gather themselves to flee. (32) As yet shall he remain at **Nob** that day: he shall shake his hand against the **mount of the daughter of Zion, the hill of Jerusalem**.

The question arises as to why Israel allows Asshur to approach Jerusalem without a fight. First of all, they have a covenant with him that should exclude them from his campaign. This is the covenant that is disannulled in Isaiah 28:18. Second, Asshur approaches from the territory known today as the West Bank. All the villages and towns described in the biblical account are in the West Bank. The West Bank is not currently under direct Israeli control. It must be noted that the area is not known in scripture as the West Bank but rather as Judea. Those who live in Judea are told in Luke 21:20–22 that they should flee to the mountains when they see Jerusalem encompassed about by armies.

<u>Descriptive Summary of Isaiah 10</u>

1. The time of the fulfillment of this prophecy is when the entire world is under the control of one man called the Assyrian and the remnant of the Jewish people are returning to the land of Israel. The timing is yet in the future. Verses 14 and 20.

2. There will be a nation of Assyria existing at some time in the future. Verse 12.

3. Israel will put their trust in Asshur to be their peace, but the agreement is broken. Verse 20.

4. Asshur is given a charge (order) to come against Israel and to be the rod of the Lord's anger. Verses 5 and 6.

5. The prophecy describes the chastisement of Israel for her sin. Verses 1–4.

6. Asshur has his own agenda and greatly distorts the Lord's directions. He gathers and conquers the whole Earth. Verses 7–14.

7. Asshur is arrogant and will be punished by the Lord. Verses 12–14.

8. Asshur's army is defeated by the Lord. Verses 16–19.

9. Asshur will stage his attack on Jerusalem from Judea, the West Bank. Verses 28–32.

<u>Isaiah 23</u>

<u>The Burden of Tyre</u>

The term "burden" means a prophecy of doom and destruction. The prophecy is directed to the coastal city of Tyre, which has also been known as Tyrus. The prophecy also includes Sidon or Zidon, another coastal port city near Tyre. Most references to these cities consider them to be a region or district. The region is mentioned many times in the New Testament and is referenced as a departure point for sea voyages in the book of Acts. The city has been conquered and laid siege to many times through history—three times by Assyrian kings between 720 BC and 663 BC, once by the Babylonian Nebuchadnezzar II, even by

Alexander the Great in 337 BC, and the latest by the Crusader Baldwin I in AD 1112.

It is important for us to know when this prophecy was or will be fulfilled. First, the destruction does not come from any other country or nation. We are told that destruction comes from the Lord.

> (8) Who hath taken this counsel against Tyre, the crowning city, whose merchants are princes, whose traffickers are the honourable of the earth? (9) The LORD of hosts hath purposed it, to stain the pride of all glory, to bring into contempt all the honourable of the earth.

Sometimes the Lord will use other nations to bring judgment to a nation, but it seems in the case of Tyre the Lord uses the sea!

> (4) Be thou ashamed, O Zidon: **for the sea hath spoken, even the strength of the sea,** saying I travail not, nor bring forth children, neither do I nourish up young men, nor bring up virgins.

This account of the destruction of this coastal area of Tyre, Zidon, and Gaza is echoed in Jeremiah 47:2,

> (2) Thus saith the LORD; Behold, **waters rise up from the north, and shall be an overflowing flood, and shall overflow the land,** and all that is therein; the city, and them that dwell therein: then the men shall cry, and all the inhabitants of the land shall howl.

(Note: the scriptures subsequent to verse 2 indicate an occupying army also enters the area after the flood.)

Until recently, to suggest that the sea could devastate a coastal city or several cities would be considered unlikely at best. But after seeing the massive devastation of an entire coastline affecting four nations and killing at least 225,000 people by the Asian Tsunami of 2004, we do not doubt the power of the sea.

Verse 1 states that "Tyre is laid waste, so that there is no house, no entering in: from the land of Chittim it is revealed to them." This statement seems to indicate that the source of that which lays Tyre waste comes from Chittim. Chittim is generally believed to be a term for the islands of the sea. So, both Tyre and Zidon, which are twenty-five miles apart are destroyed from the sea.

It is clear that this event has not yet happened. It is a future event. Both cities and the coast are intact today.

It is stated in verses 15–18 that Tyre will be forgotten for seventy years and then the Lord will visit Tyre and restore her. She will go back to her merchandizing ways, except now she will be holiness to the Lord! This is not the way it is in Tyre and Zidon today; this extraordinary transformation has yet to take place.

> (15) And it shall come to pass in that day, that **Tyre shall be forgotten seventy years**, according to the days of one king: **after the end of seventy years shall Tyre sing as an harlot**. (16) Take an harp, go about the city, thou harlot that hast been forgotten; make sweet melody, sing many songs, that thou mayest be remembered. (17) And it shall come to pass **after the end of seventy years, that the Lord will visit Tyre**, and she shall turn to her hire, and shall commit fornication with all the kingdoms of the world upon the face of the earth. (18) And **her merchandise and her hire shall be holiness to the LORD**: it shall not be treasured nor laid up; for her merchandise shall be for them that dwell before the LORD, to eat sufficiently, and for durable clothing.

To give us some more understanding concerning why Tyre and Zidon will come into conflict with the Lord we can look at Joel 3:1–4

> (1) For, behold, **in those days, and in that time, when I (the Lord) shall bring again the captivity of Judah and Jerusalem**, (2) **I will also gather all nations, and will bring them down into the valley of Jehoshaphat, and will plead with them there for my people and for my heritage Israel, whom they have scattered among the nations, and parted my land.** (3) And they have cast lots for my people; and have given a boy for

an harlot, and sold a girl for wine, that they might drink. (4) Yea, and **what have ye to do with me, O Tyre and Zidon, and all the coasts of Palestine? will ye render me a recompence**? and if ye recompence me, swiftly and speedily will **I return your recompence upon your own head**;

This passage refers to the time when God will restore the Jewish people back to their homeland in Judah and Jerusalem. He confronts the nations because they have mistreated them and have divided Israel into small pieces. The Lord specifically speaks to Tyre and Zidon and the coasts of Palestine and asks, are you trying to get even with me? "render me a recompence?" What is it that God has done that Tyre and Zidon dislike so much? He is restoring Israel his heritage to the land. They refuse to accept Israel's right to exist and God's right to give the land to the Jews. God will deal with Tyre and Zidon and also the coasts of Palestine (Gaza). Today, we find them fighting against Israel and attacking Lebanon and Gaza with missiles on a daily basis.

The fulfillment of Joel 3 is clarified in verse:

(15) The sun and the moon shall be darkened, and the stars shall withdraw their shining.

These are the same signs that Jesus says will signal the end of the age (Matthew 24:29).

Having placed the events of Isaiah 23 and Joel 3 in the end times it makes it easier to understand that the Assyrian who is referred to in Isaiah 23:13, is not an historic Assyrian, but rather the same man which we find in Micah 5 and Isaiah 10.

(13) Behold the land of the Chaldeans; **this people [nation] was not,** till **the Assyrian founded it for them** that **dwell in the wilderness**: they set up the towers thereof, they raised up the palaces thereof; and **he brought it to ruin**.

In today's world, the terms Chaldean and Assyrian have become synonymous—they are the same people but with a different church affiliation. Since 1918, the Assyrian people have been in the wilderness:

Diaspora. The term wilderness means "dry places." The plains of Nineveh are not deserts; they are fertile plains a well-watered land. The dry places where the people are coming from are the nations of the world where the Assyrian people have run for safety. The Assyrian who founds (establishes) it for them will be a modern man who will step forward and organize the restoration movement. He is the same man who becomes the king. It also says he will be responsible for Assyria's early prosperity and reconstruction, but he will also bring about the eventual ruin of the nation. It must be noted that after the Assyrian is removed by God. The Lord restores Assyria and establishes her as the work of his hands.

Descriptive Summary of Isaiah 23

1. God will destroy the coasts of Tyre and Zidon in the last days. Verses 8 and 9

2. He will use the sea to destroy the cities. Verses 1 and 4

3. God will restore Tyre and Zidon after seventy years, and they will be holy before the Lord. Verses 15–18

4. There will be an Assyrian who will found a restored nation of Assyria in the last days. He will do this for the Assyrian people living in the wilderness. He will also be responsible for Assyria's ruin. Verse 13.

Isaiah 14

"I will break the Assyrian in my land"

Chapter 14 is a continuation of chapter 13 that is a prophecy of doom, a burden, for the land of Babylon. It is a destruction that takes place at the end of the age, the time of the end. This is shown in 13:10 and 11

> (10) For the stars of heaven and the constellations thereof shall not give their light: **the sun shall be darkened in his going forth, and the moon shall not cause her light to shine.** (11) **And I will punish the world for their evil**, and the wicked for their iniquity;

Isaiah 14 starts by explaining the Lords plan for Israel in that day. It is very much the same as we have read in the accounts of Micah 5, Isaiah 10, and Joel 3. The Lord will bring them back into their land and give them rest.

> (1) **For the LORD will have mercy on Jacob, and will yet choose Israel, and set them in their own land**: and the strangers shall be joined with them, and they shall cleave to the house of Jacob. (2) And the people shall take them, and bring them to their place: and the house of Israel shall possess them in the land of the LORD for servants and handmaids: and they shall take them captives, whose captives they were; and they shall rule over their oppressors. (3) **And it shall come to pass in that day that the LORD shall give thee rest from thy sorrow, and from thy fear, and from the hard bondage wherein thou wast made to serve**,

This account indicates that not everyone will fight the Lord's will concerning the Jews and the land. They will cooperate with the Lord rather than attempt to render a recompense to the Lord after the manner of Tyre, Zidon, and Gaza.

This chapter describes events around the demise of a world leader who is being judged by the Lord. It seems he is no ordinary leader. His exploits made the earth to tremble.

> (6) **He who smote the people in wrath** with a continual stroke, **he that ruled the nations in anger**, is persecuted, and none hindereth. (7) **The whole earth is at rest**, and is quiet: they break forth into singing. (8) Yea, the fir trees rejoice at thee, and the cedars of Lebanon, saying, since thou art laid down, no feller is come up against us.

This world leader controlled the whole earth and when he meets his demise the whole sings, you might say they can peep with out fear of being smote. You can feel the relief of all the nation at being released from his control. He is in fact not only persecuted but is killed and taken to Hell.

> (9) Hell from beneath is moved for thee to meet thee at thy coming: it stirreth up the dead for thee, even all the chief ones of the earth; it has raised up from there thrones all the kings of the nations. (10) All they shall speak and say to thee, Art thou become weak as we? **art thou become like unto us**? (11) Thy pomp is brought down to the grave, and the noise of thy viols: the worm is spread under thee, and the worms cover thee… (15) Yet thou shalt be brought down to hell, **to the sides of the pit**. (16) They that see thee shall narrowly look upon thee, and consider thee saying, Is this **the man** that made the earth to tremble, and did shake the kingdoms; (17) **That made the world as a wilderness, and destroyed the cities thereof**; that opened not the house of his prisoners?

What an amazing account this is! We see beyond the natural world into the spirit world and how this man is received into Hell itself. His victims seem to be amazed that he was mortal! They question, "art thou become like us?" His pomp and pride is brought down to the sides of the pit. The extent of his destruction while he was alive is revealed— he made the world a wilderness and destroyed entire cities and never showed mercy to his enemies. He is also judged more harshly because he caused his own land and people to be destroyed.

> (20) Thou shall not be joined with them in burial, **because thou hast destroyed thy land, and slain thy people**:

If these accounts are not just allegorical but relate to spiritual realities, then we can see that there is an existence beyond the grave. And also that people have memories of their lives and are very much aware that they are dead and in Hell. Not only do the righteous have eternal life but also the wicked.

There is another account in scripture, which is related to the nations and their future abode in Hell. It gives insight as to why God judges the nation so harshly. It is found in Ezekiel 32:21–30.

(21) The strong among the mighty shall speak to him out of the midst of hell with them that help him: they are gone down, they lie uncircumcised, slain by the sword. (22) **Asshur** is there and all her company: his graves are about him: all of them slain, fallen by the sword: (23) Whose graves are **set in the sides of the pit**, and her company is round about her grave: all of them slain, fallen by the sword, **which caused terror in the land of the living.**

This account continues in verses 24–30, giving account for many nations and their part in Hell and also that they are there because they caused terror in the land of the living. The nations that are mentioned are as follows: Elam (Iran), Meshech, Tubal, (Russia), and Edom (Jordan). , The princes of the north, Zidonians (Lebanon) and Egypt, were nations seen by God as "uncircumcised" and terrorist all.

Just a few verses further on in Isaiah 14, we are able to identify who this king is.

(24) The LORD of hosts hath sworn, saying, Surely as I have thought, so shall it come to pass; and as I have purposed, so shall it stand: (25) That **I will break the Assyrian in my land, and upon my mountains** tread him under foot: then shall his yoke depart from off them, and his burden depart from off their shoulders. (26) **This is the purpose that is purposed upon the whole earth**: and this is the hand that is stretched out upon all the nations.

Yes this king is Asshur the Assyrian, and he is destroyed in the Lord's land, Israel, specifically Judea. And The mountains are the mountains round about Jerusalem!

Isaiah 14 can be a challenge to understand because the Assyrian is not the only person being referred to in the account. In verse 12 reference is made to Lucifer.

(12) How art thou fallen from heaven, **O Lucifer**, son of the morning! how art thou cut down to the ground, which didst weaken the nations! (13) For thou hast said in thine heart, **I**

will ascend into heaven, **I will** exalt my throne above the stars of God: **I will** sit also upon the mount of the congregation, in the sides of the north: (14) **I will** ascend above the heights of the clouds; **I will be like the most High**.

Lucifer is an angel, a fallen angel who was removed from heaven for his pride and rebellion. He is a spiritual being, not a man. He is the spiritual power and the source behind the Assyrian and his hatred for mankind. It is Lucifer's agenda that the Assyrian is implementing. The Assyrian and Lucifer are so closely linked that they receive the same attributes and descriptions, they are referred to as "one." They are both going to the sides of the pit. It should not surprise anyone that Lucifer is also known as Satan.

Descriptive Summary of Isaiah 14

1. Isaiah 14 is an end-time prophecy and has not yet been fulfilled. Verses 10, 11.

2. The Assyrian is shown to be a man of anger and rules all the nations in wrath with a continual stroke. Verses 6, 7.

3. The Assyrian and the Lucifer are linked together by purpose and their attributes. They work together to destroy mankind and the world. Verses 6–8, 12–14.

4. Asshur's demise and death is described, and his arrival in Hell is shown. The Lord will break the Assyrian in the land of Israel. Verses 10, 11, 15–17, 25.

5. Asshur will not remain with the other nations and the uncircumcised but will go to another location because he destroyed his own people and his own land. Verse 20.

Isaiah 30

"Tophet is ordained of old"

This chapter is primarily about the Lord's displeasure with the children of Israel for not leaning on him in the time of need and going to other nations instead.

(1) Woe to the rebellious children, saith the LORD, that take counsel. But not of me; and that cover with a covering, **but not of my spirit**, that they may add sin to sin:

It is in the heart of God and his desire to put things right with his people. God will be gracious to them and let them dwell safely in Jerusalem. This is the common end-time theme that we see from God concerning the Jewish people.

(18) And therefore will the LORD wait, that he may be gracious unto you, and therefore will he be exalted, that he may have mercy upon you: **for the LORD is a God of judgment**: blessed are all they that wait for him. (19) **For the people shall dwell in Zion at Jerusalem: thou shalt weep no more**: he will be very gracious unto thee at the voice of thy cry: when he shall hear it, he will answer thee.

The other main theme of end time prophecy is the judgment of the nations and their king, the Assyrian.

(27) Behold the name of the LORD cometh from far, burning with his anger, and the burden thereof is heavy: his lips are full of indignation, and his tongue as a devouring fire: (28) And his breath as an overflowing stream, shall reach to the midst of the neck, **to sift the nations with the sieve of vanity**: and there shall be a bridle in the jaws of the people, causing them to err... (31) For **through the voice of the LORD shall the Assyrian be beaten down, which smote with a rod.**

God will expose the vanity of the nations; this is their pride and independence from God. The Lord will allow them to think and act the way they want and their vanity will cause them to err. Today most of the experts of our time don't consider the Lord and his scriptures a viable source of wisdom; his wisdom simply doesn't apply to our modern time. We in America have what our experts call separation of church and state. This is actually a statement of separation of wisdom and Government, and it shows in the confusion that permeates the system. This situation will continue and get worse as time goes on.

The Assyrian spoken of in this chapter is the same Assyrian king we see in the previous chapters of Isaiah and Micah. He is the one who *smites with the rod*. But as has been the case throughout scripture, the Lord himself will beat him down.

This chapter ends with reference to a place called Tophet. Tophet is the name of the valley on the south side of Jerusalem. It is also called Gehenna, which means the valley of Hinnom and was the location for the disposal of garbage, dead animals, and the bodies of criminals. It was a place that always had a fire burning. The word Tophet means "place of fire." Tophet is equivalent to hell. In the New Testament, Hades or at least one chamber of it; is a lake of fire, which is most likely, a reference to Tophet.

> (33) For **Tophet is ordained of old**; yea, **for the king it is prepared**; he [the Lord] hath made it deep and large: the pile thereof is fire and much wood; the breath of the LORD, like a stream of brimstone, doth kindle it.

God has prepared Hell for the coming of the king. Specifically, the king called the Assyrian! The Lord himself has provided the fuel and has kindled the fire. The Lord has ordained this event; it will come to pass; it is not an option: the Assyrian will go to Hell.

Descriptive Summary of Isaiah 30

1. The Lord will deal with Israel's sin, but will also be gracious to it and restore them to Jerusalem. Verses 1, 18, 19.

2. The Lord judges the nations for their sin and vanity. God gives them over to their own devises and errors until God comes in indignation. Verses 27, 28

3. The Assyrian will be beaten down by the voice of the Lord. The Assyrian is identified as the one who smote with the rod. Verse 31.

4. The Assyrian is shown to be a king, not just a general or great leader. Verse 33.

5. The Lord has prepared Tophet, the place of fire, Hell, for the Assyrian. The Lord has ordained his demise. Verse 33.

Isaiah 31
Be afraid of the ensign

Isaiah 31 is only nine verses long, yet much is found therein. Israel is again chided for not looking to the Lord for their help. It states that Israel deeply revolted, but the Lord still defends and delivers Jerusalem.

> (5) As birds flying, **so will the LORD of hosts defend Jerusalem**; **defending also he will deliver it**; and passing over he will preserve it, (6) Turn ye unto him (the Lord) from whom the children of **Israel have deeply revolted**.

Israel's revolt from God is not a slight thing; the term revolt means they defected from trusting and serving God. It was a deep and profound choice that they made to trust man. The result of the Lord dealing with Israel is that a day will come when they will cast away their Idols of gold and silver, which they made with their own hands. It isn't until they see a total lack of value in the things they've made that they can throw them away.

> (7) For **in that day** every man shall cast away his idols of silver, and his idols of gold, which your own hands have made unto you for a sin,

Reference to the Assyrian comes in verse 8 and speaks to his death. We've read in previous chapters that the Assyrian dies and goes to Hell, but this account gives some specifics that we've not see before. It states that he is killed or falls with the sword. The Hebrew word means a knife or dagger. The wound was not received in battle nor from one of his enemies. He was not killed by a mighty man, a soldier, but by an ordinary man. Obviously, he did not expect this man to attack him. Asshur had actually withdrawn from the battlefield because of fear. He had retreated back to a stronghold—a place he felt safe. He had fled because he saw the Lord's ensign. This ensign had caused him and his princes to be afraid. He retreated leaving his young soldiers to be defeated: the term is "discomfited," which means to pay a price. This may be the first time his armies have tasted defeat.

> (8) **Then shall the Assyrian fall with the sword**, not of a mighty man; and the sword not of a mean man, shall devour him: but he shall flee from the sword, and his young men shall be discomfited. (9) And **he shall pass over to his strong hold for fear**, and his princes shall be **afraid of the ensign**, saith the LORD, whose fire is in Zion and his furnace in Jerusalem.

The reference to the fire in Zion and his furnace in Jerusalem is the fire of Tophet, which God has ordained for the Assyrian's death.

Descriptive Summary of Isaiah 31

1. Israel is judged for their rebellion from the Lord. Verse 6.
2. The Lord defends and delivers Jerusalem. Verse 5.
3. Asshur falls by the sword. He is killed, and the fire is prepared for him. Verse 8.
4. Asshur's armies are defeated and are afraid of the Lord's ensign, his war banner which flies before his army.

CHAPTER TWO

Asshur and Persia

The obvious relationship between Assyria and Persia is one of geographic location; they are neighbors. Northern Persia and Assyria border each other or at least are very near. The modern nation of Iran is actually the ancient nation of Persia. Iran today encompasses more than old Persia. Iran is a large nation and probably includes some of old Media, Assyria, and certainly all of Ancient Elam.

There is in scripture a connection of far greater significance than just geographic location. The prophet Daniel is given information that will apply to the times in which we are now living. Daniel 10 gives an account concerning future kings and leaders that will come from Persia. This account comes from a messenger sent from God to Daniel.

> (5) Then I lifted up mine eyes, and looked, and behold a certain man clothed in linen, whose loins were girded with fine gold of Uphaz: (6) His body also was like the beryl, and his face like as the appearance of lightning, and his eyes as lamps of fire, and his arms and his feet like the colour of polished brass, and the voice of his words like the voice of a multitude.

At the sight of this messenger, Daniel basically collapses and is unable to deal with what he was seeing. The messenger helps Daniel to regain some of his composure and begins to explain why he had come and what his message is about.

> (14) Now I am come to make thee understand what shall befall

thy people in the latter days: for yet **the vision is for many days**.

It is important to know that the information concerns Israel and the Jewish people even though most of the vision seems to be about Persia and kings, which will rise up from there. The vision continues in chapter 11. We will start in verse 2.

(2) And now will I shew thee the truth. Behold there shall stand up **yet three kings in Persia**; and **the fourth shall be far richer than they all**:

The rise and fall of these kings are described in this chapter. The first king is seen in verse 3, the second in verse 7, and the third in verse 20. These first three kings are not the focus of this study—it is the fourth king that is of interest. His story starts in verse 21:

(21) And in his [the third king's] estate shall stand up **a vile person**,[the fourth king] to whom **they shall not give the honour of the kingdom**: but **he shall come in peaceably**, and obtain the kingdom by flatteries.

We are told he is a man of peace and is not above using flatteries to get his way. The word used for flattery has the connotation of being smooth; he is a smooth talker. Flattery is also a tool to reach out to a person's pride and arrogance. He is not the first choice to be king. He is not given the honor and can't be the king, but his ambition and desire will at some point win the day. He is also considered to be vile.

(22) And with the arms of a flood shall they be overflown from before him, and shall be broken; yea, also the prince of the covenant.

This shows that he will use military power to get his way. He will come with overwhelming power, like a flood, and shall break his enemies. He will also fight against the prince of the covenant, the Lord himself. This king is truly vile.

> (23) And after the league made with him he shall work deceitfully: for he shall come up, and shall become strong with **a small people**. (24) He shall **enter peaceably** even upon the fattest places of the province; and he shall do that which his fathers have not done, nor his fathers' fathers; **he shall scatter among them the prey, and spoil, and riches**: yea and he shall forecast his devices against the strong holds, even for a time.

This man is shown to be dishonest. He starts out as a man of peace but soon is using deceit to get his way. He also breaks with the traditions of his fathers and does things they would not approve of. He scatters among the people the riches of his activities to secure their support. The general public will turn a blind eye to his deceit if they benefit from it, and they will in effect be paid off.

He is able to move into territories without resistance: "enter peaceably even upon the fattest places of the province." It says he will "forecast his devices against the strong holds." This term "forecast" means to cast a spell. A spell is a spiritual exercise to get a desired result. He will speak into the spirit realm to receive spiritual help to defeat his enemies and pull down strong holds. The term "strong holds" speaks beyond just natural fortifications into spiritual defenses.

In 2 Corinthians 10:4, the Christians are told that they have spiritual power through prayer to God to pull down strong holds.

> (4) For the weapons of our warfare are not carnal, but mighty through God to the pulling down of strong holds.

This king will have an understanding of the need to fight his battles in the spirit realm as well as the natural. He will turn to spells instead of God and will only be successful for a time. The term "his devices" refers to his "desires." He wants to have his way, and he will not submit to anyone, not even the prince of the covenant.

The word "league," which is found in verse 23, means a compact or agreement made as a result of a spell or charm, but we know it is the work of deceit and lies that the king has no intent to honour it. Also in this verse is found an interesting fact: he will become strong with a

31

small people. The term "people" means "nation." He will not receive his power from Persia, which is a large, strong nation, but rather will be the king of a small nation. He will use this power platform to extend his power beyond to other nations.

Verses 25 through 30 describe some negotiations and series of military campaigns between this king and the king of the south. The king of the south is understood to be Egypt, based on other scriptural references and its relationship to the land of Israel. The negotiations are found in verse 27:

> (27) And **both these kings' hearts shall be to do mischief**, and **they shall speak lies at one table**; but it shall not prosper: for yet the end shall be at the time appointed.

Wicked leaders use negotiations as tools to disarm an opponent and get them to relax their guard. In this example, both kings intend to destroy the other. The vile king gets the advantage and destroys the king of the south:

> (25) **and he [vile king] shall stir up his power and his courage against the king of the south with a great army**; and the king of the south shall be stirred up to battle with a very great and mighty army; **but he [king of the south] shall not stand**: for they shall forecast devices against him. (26) Yea, they that feed of the portion of his meat shall destroy him, and his army shall overflow: and many shall fall down slain. (28) Then shall he [the vile king] return to his land with great riches; and **his heart shall be against the holy covenant**; and he shall do exploits, and **return to his own land**.

The king's heart is turned against the Lord and the Lord's covenant with his people. The covenant spoken of is with the Jewish people, but Christians have been grafted in to the covenant (Romans 11:17). In order for a Christian to be against the holy covenant he would be apostate, forsaking the very foundation of his faith.

> (29) **At the time appointed he [the vile king] shall return, and come towards the south**; but it shall **not be as the**

former, or as the latter. (30) For the **ships of Chittim shall come against him**: therefore he shall be grieved, and return, and have **indignation against the holy covenant**: so shall he do; he shall even return, and have **intelligence with them that forsake the holy covenant**.

After destroying and spoiling Egypt, the king decides to go towards the south. This is not Egypt as before, "the former," but would be the land of the holy covenant, Israel. But the navy of Chittim intervenes against this campaign and turns him back. The king is outraged at the outcome and sets about making a plan to deal with Chittim. Chittim is a nation of the sea, which has a navy capable of preventing a ground assault. Only modern navies have the weapons to accomplish this. Probably only one nation today could do this—the United States.

Asshur turns to those nations who have forsaken the holy covenant. It is impossible to forsake something you had never accepted. They would-be nations which were at least nominally Christian, non-Moslem, and probably European. Russia could be included as an apostate Christian nation. With the help of his allies, he removes Chittim and its navy from his way. He takes his armies and goes into the holy land and takes Jerusalem.

(31) And arms [armies] shall stand on his part, and **they shall pollute the sanctuary** of strength [Jewish temple], and take away the daily sacrifice, and **they shall place the abomination that maketh desolate**.

This vile king is Asshur. Asshur places the abomination of desolation in the temple and is the king that controls Jerusalem. The small people (nation) from whom he raises is in fact Assyria, the post-Diaspora restored nation of the end times. The abomination of desolation is why this prophecy is about the Jews and Israel.

Even though the king is ethnically Assyrian, he comes to prominence from Persia, which is modern Iran. He will be a citizen of Iran not Iraq and will later lead the Assyrian people to become a nation again (he founded it for them). It is also clear that the Assyrians armies are actually from many different nations, not just Assyrians. It is also clear why by forsaking the holy covenant he is doing things his fathers have never done. Asshur's heritage is Christian. and he will turn from it to serve another god.

> (37) Neither shall he regard the **God of his fathers**, nor the desire of women, nor regard any god: **for he shall magnify himself above all**. (38) But in his estate shall he honour the **God of forces**: and **a god whom his fathers knew not shall he honour with gold**, and silver, and with precious stones, and pleasant things. (39) **Thus shall he do in the most strong holds with a strange god**, whom he shall acknowledge and increase with glory: and he shall cause them to rule over many, and shall divide the land for gain.

The God of forces, who is mentioned, is actually the God of fortresses, who is the god of Nimrod the first king after the great flood. This god was called Bel, the bright one, the sun-like god. He is known scripturally as Lucifer and Satan an angel of Phos (light).

But, while he will give Satan credit for his wealth and prosperity, he will not bow to him because he believes himself to be divine and to be god. He worships himself above all.

Asshur will continue to rule and prosper for a short time after taking Jerusalem, because the end is not yet. He will be free to do what ever he wants until God's indignation shall come to pass.

> (36) And the king shall do according to his will; and he shall exalt himself, and **magnify himself above every god**, and shall speak marvellous things against the God of gods, and **shall prosper till the indignation be accomplished**: for that which is determined shall be done.

Verses 32–35 diverge from speaking about the Assyrian and his campaigns and move to the plight and exploits of those in Judea who flee directly from Asshur and his armies. We know these are Jews because the messenger told us that this is what will befall Daniels' people in the later days.

(32) And such as do wickedly against the covenant shall he [the Assyrian] **corrupt by flatteries**: but the people that do know their God shall be strong and do exploits. (33) And **they that understand** among the people shall instruct many: **yet they shall fall by the sword, and by flame, by captivity, and by spoil**, many days. (34) Now when they shall fall, they shall be holpen with a little help: but many shall cleave to them with flatteries. (35) **And some of them of understanding shall fall, to try them, and to purge, and to make them white, even to the time of the end**: because it is yet for a time appointed.

Asshur is not a man of mercy. He is very hard on those who oppose him. He is full of hatred for the Jews. He will kill by the sword (executions), by the flame. This a chilling thought after what the Nazis did in World War II. As to captivity, he will use prisons and spoil. A spoil is an economic action. Asshur will destroy and control people financially.

When they fall into his hands, there is very little that can be done to help. We should remember that this is the time that the Lord will do a whole work in Zion (Isaiah 10:12). God will be dealing with his people for good. Some will fall to try them, to test them, to purge out anything God does not want. The Lord will make them white, that is, righteous. This is the complete opposite of what is happening to nations around them. They are going further into perdition and closer to God's wrath.

The Armageddon Sequence
"He shall come to his end and none shall help"

The remaining verses of this chapter, 40-45, are an amazing account of the events surrounding the Assyrian and Israel. They chronicle these events and give a sequence that allows us to better understand these events. The war between God and the nations, which is fought over Israel's' right to exist and live in the land given to them by God, is commonly called Armageddon. It is not a single battle but rather a series of military campaigns centered around Israel and Assyrian.

It needs to be understood that Israel and the Assyrian have an agreement for the protection of Israel. Whenever a nation threatens or attacks Israel, it is as though they are attacking or challenging Asshur's power and authority. They are pushing against him. This agreement is the "stay," which the Lord is so angry about. It will be annulled at the point when the Asshur turns against the holy covenant and moves into Jerusalem. Both Israel and Asshur move militarily in some of these battles. In other prophecies, we also find the accounts of God's intervention and participation in these battles. For references to Egypt read Ezekiel 29; for Russia, Ezekiel 38 and 39.

> Daniel 11:40: And at the time of the end shall the king of the south push at him:…

This is the first campaign. We read earlier in this chapter how this battle goes down. The land of Egypt is defeated and spoiled. Verse 40 continues:

> ….and the king of the north shall come against him like a whirlwind, with chariot, and with horsemen, and with many ships;….

This is the second campaign. The king of the north is believed to be Russia. Russia is seen coming into Israel in the last days and suffers a tremendous defeat. This account is seen in Ezekiel 38 and 39. Verse 40 continues:

> ….and he [the Assyrian] shall enter in the countries, and shall overflow and pass over.

This is the third campaign. With Russia and Egypt destroyed, he is able to move into other nations, probably Eastern Europe and the old Soviet Union. We know that he joins or aligns himself with some nominally Christian nations in the north. He is consolidating his power base in the north.

> (41) He [the Assyrian] shall enter also into **the glorious land**, and many countries shall be overthrown: but these shall escape

out of his hand, even **Edom, and Moab**, and the chief of the children of **<u>Ammon</u>**.

This is the fourth campaign. He moves into Israel, the glorious land. At this time, he breaks his agreement with Israel and invades Jerusalem. We have seen many accounts of this campaign in Isaiah and Micah. He does not stop or restrict himself to Israel but overthrows many countries in the Middle East. For some reason he does not continue into modern Jordan, which is Edom, Moab, and Ammon. It so happens that this area is the location that those in Judea are told to flee to when they see Jerusalem surrounded by armies.

(44) But tidings [news] out of the east and out of the north shall trouble him: therefore he [the Assyrian] shall go forth with **<u>great fury to destroy, and utterly make away many</u>**.

The fifth campaign is the news that the kings of the east are coming, and he goes out to meet them in battle. The kings of the east are part of the sixth vial of God's wrath poured out by the sixth angel found in Revelation 16:12. This event is related to the gathering of the nations to place of Armageddon for the great day of God (Revelation 16:14 and 16). Revelation 9:13 and 14 speak of a two-hundred-million man army coming across the Euphrates River from the east. The Assyrian can only be using weapons of mass destruction to stop an army of this size.

By the time this campaign takes place, it will be clear to the entire world that the Assyrian will not be content until he rules and controls the entire world. This frightening reality is what will motivate the kings of the east, China, Japan, and India to march headlong into this slaughter.

The sixth campaign is news (tidings) from the north. This cannot be Russia, because she was destroyed in campaign two. This is an internal rebellion from within his northern or European confederacy. He moves quickly to destroy the rebels and put down the rebellion. This will be studied in detail in later chapters of this book under the subject of "the little horn." Daniel 7:20 tells us that three kings will fall and be plucked up.

(45) And he shall plant the tabernacles of his palace between the seas in the **glorious holy mountain**; yet **shall he come to his end, and none shall help him**.

This is the seventh and final campaign. The Assyrian meets his demise when the Lord and his army enters Israel from Edom and destroys Asshur's army. We know from our study of Isaiah that the Asshur dies by the sword and is taken to Hell.

Descriptive Summary of Daniel 10 and 11

1. This vision is delivered to Daniel by a messenger sent from God. Daniel 10:5 and 6.

2. The vision pertains to Daniel's people, the Jews, and what will happen to them in the last days. Daniel 10:14.

3. There will be four kings coming up from within Persia. The fourth king is different than the first three. Verse 2.

4. The fourth king attacks Jerusalem and places the abomination of desolation in the holy place (Jewish temple). He is the same person as the Assyrian (Asshur) of Isaiah's prophecies. Verse 31.

5. This king is ethnically Assyrian but also is a Persian citizen and comes to prominence in Persia (modern Iran), but he gets his kingdom from a small nation, the modern restored Assyria. Verse 23.

6. This Assyrian king will also be the leader of a multinational confederacy of nations, some from Europe and some from the Middle East. Verse 30.

7. Asshur will attack and destroy the king of the south, Egypt. Verse 25.

8. Asshur will set himself up to be worshiped as God. He will also honor Lucifer (the god of fortresses) and forsake the holy covenant. Verses 28, 38 and 39.

9. The last four verses of this chapter are a concise synopsis of the movements and military campaigns pertaining to Israel and Asshur.

There is a sequence of seven battles that make up what is commonly known as Armageddon. Verses 40–45.

10. Asshur eliminates the navy of Chittim, the islands of the sea. Verse 30.

CHAPTER THREE

Asshur and the Little Horn

The book of Daniel has several chapters that deal with the end times and a man called the little horn. Many times in scripture, God uses the symbol of a horn to represent kings. This is true in both Old and New Testaments. The first account in Daniel is the seventh chapter. Daniel had a dream and visions on his bed. He saw four great beasts coming up from the great sea (Mediterranean), and they were each different. The first was like a lion, the second a bear, and the third was a leopard. These first three beasts are very interesting but are not directly relevant to this study about Asshur, so we will not go into detail concerning them. However, the fourth beast is important and revealing.

> (7) After this I saw in the night visions, and behold **a fourth beast**, dreadful and terrible, and strong exceedingly; and it had great iron teeth: it devoured and brake in pieces, and stamped the residue with the feet of it: and it was diverse from all the beasts that were before it; and it had **ten horns**.

It is amazing to me how God is able to take the qualities and characteristics of a kingdom and visually display and describe them as a beast or animal. This beast is said to be dreadful—when you see it you will want to instantly run the other way, and you hope that you will never have to see or face it again. It has great iron teeth; it is like a great machine that has the strength to move forward no matter what is in its way. It stamps with its feet what it chews with its teeth. This is an awesome display of unbridled anger. Its entire purpose is that of destruction. It wants to kill and destroy. The ten horns show that this beast is not just one nation, but a group or confederacy of ten nations.

> (8) I considered the horns, and, behold there came up among them **another little horn**, before whom there were **three of the first horns plucked up by the roots**: and, behold, in this horn were eyes like the **eyes of man, and a mouth speaking great things**.

While Daniel was contemplating the ten horns, another comes up from among them. He is a small horn, but although small, he will puck up three of the ten by the roots. It is clear that he becomes their leader. He is a small king, probably not small in stature, but from a small kingdom or nation. However, he does not have a small ego or ambitions. He takes over the strongest military confederacy of nations in existence at that time. He is the eleventh king.

Daniel was so taken back by this fourth beast that later in this chapter he asks for an explanation:

> (19) Then I would know the **truth of the fourth beast**, which was **diverse** from all the others, exceeding dreadful, whose teeth were of iron, and his nails of brass; which devoured, brake in pieces, and stamped the residue with his feet; (20) And of the **ten horns** that were in his head, and of the other which came up, and **before whom three fell**; even of that horn that had eyes, and a mouth that spoke very great things, whose **look was more stout than his fellows**. (21) I beheld, and the same horn made war with the saints, and prevailed against them; (22) **Until the Ancient of days came**, and judgment was given to the saints of the most High; and the time came that the saints possessed the kingdom.
> (23) Thus he said, The fourth beast shall be the fourth kingdom upon earth, which shall be diverse from all kingdoms, and **shall devour the whole earth** and shall tread it down, and break it in pieces.

There has never been, in all of history, a kingdom like this one! It is different than all other kingdoms. It is not a continuation of another kingdom but a completely new arrangement. Only one king and one kingdom will ever conquer and rule the entire earth, and that is Asshur's. We know from previous passages that he will lead a powerful alliance of nations. We also know that Asshur destroys the earth and treads it down. He is also the king of a small people. He is this "little horn."

> (24) And the ten horns out of this kingdom are **ten kings** that shall arise: and **another shall rise after them**; and he shall be diverse from the first, and **he shall subdue three kings**.

In Daniel 11 we studied an event where the Assyrian receives tidings (a report) from the north and moves with fury to destroy someone in the north. This happens shortly after he moves into Judea and Jerusalem. This timing would be consistent with the demise of these three kings:

> (25) And he shall speak great words against the most High, and shall wear out the saints of the most High, and **think to change times and laws**: and they shall be given into his hand **until a time and times and a dividing of time**.

Because of his pride and arrogance, the little horn will have no problem speaking against God and declaring that things will be different now. The old rules and ways that God had established to be the standards of conduct and accountability are now void. The saints of the most High will be put into subjection for three and one half years, Time (one year) times (two more years) and a dividing of time (plus one half year) this equals three and one half years.

> (26) **But the judgment shall sit, and they shall take away his dominion, to consume and to destroy it unto the end**. (27) And the kingdom and dominion, and the greatness of the kingdom under the whole heaven, shall be **given to the people of the saints of the most High**, whose **kingdom is an**

everlasting kingdom, and all dominions shall serve and obey him. (28) **Hitherto is the end of the matter**....

Clearly, the little horn's kingdom, Asshur's kingdom, is the last of man's kingdoms to exist before God, the most High, sets up his everlasting kingdom. God's people are encouraged that they will be active participants in that kingdom, which will have no end! He reveals two keys to the kingdom. The first is service, and the second is obedience. Dear reader, learn to serve and obey the Lord today, and you will be his in that day, the day he calls his own home.

In verses 11 and 12 there is a truth that will help us to better understand the scriptures from the book of Revelation, which will study later in this chapter. The first three beasts of this vision are *sequential i*n their dominion, but exist *simultaneously*. The first three kingdoms continue to exist after the fourth is destroyed. This means they all exist at the same time.

(11) I beheld then because of the voice of the great words which the horn spake: I beheld even till the beast was slain, and **his body** destroyed, and given to the **burning flame**. (12) As concerning the rest of the beasts, they had their **dominion taken away**: yet their **lives were prolonged** for a season and time.

We see again that the Asshur is destined for the fire. Tophet is ordained of old for his arrival.

Descriptive Summary of Daniel 7

1. There are four kingdoms to sequentially have domination in the Middle East in the last days. Verses 2 and 3.

2. These four kingdoms lose their dominance sequentially but continue to exist simultaneously. Verses 11 and 12.

3. The forth kingdom is also a world kingdom, controlling the entire earth—the only kingdom to ever accomplish this. Verse 23.

4. The forth kingdom has ten horns, ten kings, and is ruled by an eleventh king called the little horn. Verses 7 and 8.

5. The Lord destroys the little horn when the Lord comes to set up his kingdom, an everlasting kingdom, and the little horn is sent to the flame, to Hell. Verses 11, 13, 14, and 26.

6. The little horn is the same man as the Assyrian, the one who comes from a small people.

7. The little horn, Asshur, is given dominion over the saints of the most High for three and one half years. Verse 25.

8. The little horn, the Assyrian, destroys three of the original ten kings at some time during his rule. Verse 8 and 24

Daniel 8

From them came forth a little horn

Daniel, while in captivity in the palace at Shushan in the province of Elam has a vision. He sees different animals, and each represents kings and kingdoms and again horns are also used to represent kings. The vision starts with a ram:

> (3) Then I lifted up mine eyes, and saw, and, behold, there stood before the river **a ram which had two horns**: and the two horns were high; but one was higher than the other, and the higher came up last. (4) I saw the ram pushing westward, and northward, and southward; so that no beasts might stand before him, neither was there any that could deliver out of his hand; but did according to his will, and became great.

The interpretation was given to Daniel in verse 20:

> The ram which thou sawest having two horns **are the kings of Media and Persia**.

The king of Persia which came up first is Cyrus. He is historically a great king and a high horn. He was special to the Lord, who referred to Cyrus as "my shepherd" and also as his "anointed." The second, is Darius the Mede, and he was a great king and had great accomplishments. Daniel's vision continues:

(5) And as I was considering, behold, an **he goat** came from the west on the face of the whole earth, and touched not the ground: and the goat had a notable horn between his eyes. (6) And he came to the ram that had two horns, which I had there seen standing before the river, and ran unto him in the fury of his power. (7) **And I saw him come close unto the ram, and he was moved with choler against him, and smote the ram, and brake his two horns**: and there was no power in the ram to stand before him, but he cast him down to the ground, and stamped upon him: and there was none that could deliver the ram out of his hand. (8) **Therefore the he goat waxed very great: and when he was strong, the great horn was broken; and for it came up four notable ones toward the four winds of heaven**.

The interpretation was given to Daniel in verses 21 and 22:

And **the rough goat is the king of Grecia**: and the great horn that is between his eyes is the first king. (22) **Now that being broken, whereas four stood up for it, four kingdoms shall stand up out of the nation, but not in his power**.

This king of Greece is Alexander the Great. The account fits his life, death, and the subsequent dividing of his empire by his four generals perfectly. It's worth noting that if the descriptions and accounts of these first two kingdoms are so precise, that it's only reasonable to expect the remaining descriptions to be just as accurate. The vision continues:

(9) And **out of one of them [the four] came forth a little horn**, which waxed exceeding great, toward the south, and toward the east and toward the pleasant land. (10) And it waxed great, even to the host of heaven; and it cast down some of the host and of the stars to the ground, and stamped upon them. (11) Yea, **he magnified himself even to the prince of the host**, and **by him the daily sacrifice was taken away, and the place of his sanctuary was cast down**.

The little horn is seen to be the king that takes away the daily sacrifice and defiles the sanctuary. He is Asshur, the prideful, arrogant king that defies God and exalts himself as though he is God. He will come from one the four areas of Alexander's generals. We know from our study of Daniel 11 that he is from Persia—modern Iran. How do we know that this is not some historic king? First, there is no historic record of such a king, and of course, he could not have escaped notice. However, the biggest reason is that Daniel was told it would happen at the time of the end.

(17…Understand, O son of man: for at the **time of the end** shall be the vision. (19) … I will make thee know what shall be **in the last end of the indignation**: for at the time appointed the **end shall be**.

The interpretation and explanation of the little horn further confirms his identity as Asshur.

(23) And in the latter time of their kingdom, when the transgressors are come to the full, a **king of fierce countenance**, and **understanding dark sentences**, shall stand up. (24) And his power **shall be mighty**, but **not by his own power**: and he **shall destroy wonderfully**, and shall prosper, and practice, and **shall destroy the mighty and the holy people**. (25) And through his policy also he **shall cause craft to prosper** in his hand; and **he shall magnify himself** in his heart, and **by peace shall destroy many**: he shall also stand up against the Prince of princes; but he shall be broken without hand.

The little horn will stand up when the transgressors are come to the *full*. God is longsuffering and has put off judging this world and its sin for literally thousands of years, yet there will be a time when the cup is full and God will move to end the age and the end will come. Asshur's fierceness is the result of anger, and it shows in his face. Asshur will have understanding of difficult questions and situations "dark sentences" and hidden things.

We know that he forecasts and uses spells to get direction and assistance from the spirit realm. It's not really Asshur's understanding but his spiritual intelligence gathering. He is powerful, but it's not his power. We also know that his power is from Lucifer, the angel Satan. He of course believes that it is all his doing, thus he is arrogant beyond degree. He shall destroy wonderfully. This literally means he corrupt the simple people who buy into his kingdom through signs and wonders. He will destroy the holy people because they represent the truth. They are separate (holy) from Asshur and his system, and they must be eliminated.

In Asshur's hand and through his policies business "craft" will prosper. The root of evil is the love of money, and this kingdom of transgressors will be pulled to the money he has to spread around. He uses his promise of peace to obtain power and subdue the will of the people. He will be a man of peace for a time, but for the last three and one half years he is a terror to the world. His time is limited by God. When he stands up to fight the Lord, the Prince of princes, Asshur, is broken without hand. We know he retreats to a stronghold when he sees the Lord's ensign, and he dies there.

Descriptive Summary of Daniel 8

1. Daniel had a vision about a ram with two horns. The ram represents the Medes and the Persians, and the two horns were the two historic kings Cyrus the Great and Darius. Verses 3, 4, and 20.

2. Next, Daniel saw a he goat, which had a great horn between his eyes. The he goat is shown to be Alexander the Great. He was replaced at his death by four of his top generals, and they divided up the empire into four regions. Verses 8, 21, and 22.

3. From one of the four regions of Alexander's empire come up a little horn, in the *time of the end*. The little horn removes the daily sacrifice and defiles the sanctuary. These are the acts of the fourth Persian king (Daniel 11) who is also known as the Assyrian. *The little horn is Asshur*. Verses 9, 10, and 11.

4. The Assyrian shall be mighty but not in his own power. Satan will be his source. He will also perform signs and wonders and destroy through peace. Verses 24, 25.

5. Business and commerce shall prosper in his hand and through his policies. Verse 25.

6. Asshur will magnify himself in his heart and stand up against the Lord, the Prince of princes, and shall come to his end. Verse 25.

CHAPTER FOUR

Asshur the Beast

The apostle John was in exile on Patmos when he received the Revelation from the Lord. In chapter 13, John describes a beast which he saw rise out of the sea, this is his account:

> (1) And I stood upon the sand of the sea, and saw a beast rise up out of the sea, having **seven heads and ten horns**, and upon his horns ten crowns, and upon his heads the name of blasphemy. (2) And the beast which I saw was like unto a **leopard**, and his feet were as the feet of a **bear**, and his mouth as the mouth of a **lion**: and the **dragon** gave him his power, and his seat, and great authority.

This beast has ten horns just the same as Daniel's fourth beast of Daniel 7. John's beast has absorbed the first three kingdoms: the leopard, bear, and lion. They are now a part of the fourth beast. There is reference to seven heads. These are a series of great empires ruling God's people and his land, starting with Egypt. They are as follows: Egypt, Assyria, Babylon, Medes and Persia, Greece, Rome, and finally the kingdom of ten kings. We will take a more detailed look at the seven heads later in this chapter from Revelation 17.

This beast receives his power, seat, and authority from the dragon. The dragon is not specifically identified in these verses but can be identified elsewhere. In Revelation 12, just in front of our verses, there is a wonder seen in verse 3:

(3) And there appeared another wonder in heaven; and behold a **great red dragon**, having **seven heads and ten horns**, and seven crowns upon his heads.
(9) And the great dragon was cast out, that old serpent, **called the Devil, and Satan**, which deceiveth the whole world….

It is clear who the dragon is—it is Satan himself. The seven heads and ten horns are his kingdom, and he gives it to the beast with authority, his seat and power. This kingdom is the world system, which started with Nimrod at Babel and continues until the final kingdom, which are the ten kings. This collection of heads and horns make up the "world" which Christians are told in scripture to avoid.

I John 2:15–18
(15) Love not the world, neither the things that are in the world, If any man love the world, the love of the Father is not in him. (16) For all that is in the world, the lust of the flesh, and the lust of the eyes, and the pride of life, is not of the Father, but is of the world. (17) And the world passeth away, and the lust thereof: but he that doeth the will of God abideth forever. (18) Little children, it is the last time: and as ye have heard that antichrist shall come….

John's vision continues in Revelation 13:

(3) And I saw **one of his heads** as it were **wounded to death**; and his deadly wound was healed: and all the world wondered after the beast. (4) And they [the world] **worshipped the dragon**, which gave power unto the beast: and they **worshipped the beast**, saying, who is like unto the beast? Who is able to make war with him?

There are two disturbing points found in these two verses. First, the people worship the beast. They have stooped so low as to worship a man. But, even worse, they appear to understand the source of his power, and they worship Satan as well. Granted, Satan may not appear to them as a great red dragon but rather as a great angel of light, as

Lucifer. It must also be noted that today's young people are enamored with dragons and other such creatures, which they absorb through their video games.

The reference to the wounded head of one of the seven will be discussed later in this chapter. John continues:

> (5) And there was given unto him a mouth speaking great things and blasphemies; and power was given unto him **to continue forty and two months**. (6) and he opened his mouth in blasphemy against God, to blaspheme his name, and his tabernacle, and them that dwell in heaven. (7) And it was **given unto him to make war with the saints**, and to overcome them: and **power was given him over all kindreds, and tongues, and nations**.

We know that Asshur is the king who has a world kingdom in the last days. He also controls Jerusalem for three and one half years— forty and two months. Asshur blasphemes God's tabernacle by setting himself up to be worshipped. He also makes war with God's people and does miracles with Satan's power. *The beast, the man who is given Satan's kingdom, is Asshur the Assyrian.* Who is able to make war with him or is able to peep or move the wing?

John continues:

> (8) And all that dwell upon the earth shall worship him, whose names are not written in the book of life of the Lamb slain from the foundation of the world. (9) If any man have an ear, let him hear. (10) **He that leadeth into captivity shall go onto captivity: he that killeth with the sword must be killed with the sword**. Here is the patience and the faith of the saints.

We find a distinction made between those people who stoop so low as to worship a man and those whose names are written in the lamb's book of life. The man from Bethlehem, who will be the peace when the Assyrian comes into Israel (Micah 5), will have been slain for that peace as a lamb is slain on the altar. Those who accept that sacrifice will be separated from the world before judgment comes.

He that leadeth into captivity is the beast (Asshur). He also will go into captivity, and he (Asshur) that killeth with the sword will be killed with the sword. This fact was established in Isaiah 31:8, already studied, and he goes into Hell (captivity). The reference to patience and faith is a reference back to Isaiah 10:24 and 25 in which the Lord encourages his people that a very little while, and the indignation will pass and the Assyrian's burden shall be removed from off their shoulder.

In verse 11 another beast is brought to light. He come up from out of the earth. This book is focused on studying Asshur the Assyrian, but this other beast does directly interface with Asshur so we will explore the connection.

> (11) And I beheld another beast coming up out of the earth; and he had **two horns like a lamb**, and he **spake as a dragon**. (12) And he exerciseth all the power of the first beast before him, and **causeth the earth and them which dwell therein to worship the first beast**, whose deadly wound was healed. (13) And he doeth great wonders, so that **he maketh fire come down from heaven on the earth in the sight of men**, (14) And deceiveth them that dwell on the earth by means of those miracles which he had power to do in the sight of the beast; saying to them that dwell on the earth, that they should make an image to the beast, which had the wound by the sword, and did live.(15) And he had power to give life unto the image of the beast, that the image of the beast should both speak, **and cause that as many as would not worship the image of the beast should be killed**. (16) And he causeth all, both small and great, rich and poor, free and bond, **to receive a mark in their right hand or in their foreheads**: (17) **And that no man might buy or sell, save he that had the mark, or the name of the beast, or the number of his name.**(18) Here is wisdom. Let him that hath understanding count the number of the beast, for it is the number of a man; and his number is Six hundred threescore and six.

This new beast is not found associated with Asshur anywhere in the Old Testament. These facts about Asshur's kingdom will help us to understand how he is able to so completely control and dominate all the world's kingdoms. The new beast appears to be a holy man, one who speaks for God. He is in appearance as a lamb, cloaked in the garb of a religious system, but he comes not in the power of God. He operates in all the power of the first beast. We know that power was from the dragon, Satan.

This prophet will be connected to Satan and not to God. This becomes evident when he speaks. He speaks not like the Lord but like the dragon. He is not lifting himself up but rather seems totally dedicated to promoting the Assyrian. He goes on a crusade to prove to the world that Asshur (the beast) is more that just a man and that he is worthy of worship.

The prophet is able to do great wonders and to cause great spiritual manifestations, such as fire coming from heaven. This is a counterfeit of the miracle done by Elijah on Mount Carmel against the prophets of Baal (I Kings 18). In which Satan lost 450 false prophets in one day. The prophet is very successful in deceiving the people of the earth, he convinces the people to make an image of Asshur, to honor him, and to worship the image. The worship of the beast starts during the forty-two month time period after Asshur captures Jerusalem.

Placing an image in the temple at Jerusalem would constitute the abomination of desolation spoken of by Daniel. The false prophet goes as far as to require everyone to worship the image upon penalty of death. When scripture says everyone must worship the beast, there will be no exceptions—small and great, rich and poor, free and bond, all will be subject to the false worship. There will be no separation of church and state in Asshur's government.

In order to verify a person's fidelity to the Assyrian, the false prophet requires everyone to be marked. Without the mark no one can buy or sell. This means no food and no paycheck. The mark will be received on the body, either on the forehead or right hand. The mark will vary for some reason, probably because of one's position within the kingdom or one's ethnic background. There will be just a mark without a precise definition, probably for the masses, *or* the name of the beast (a written name), or the number of his name (666).

The false prophet will not be exempt from judgment in the day of the Lord, when God sets up a kingdom, which will never end. This event is seen in Revelation 19:

> (19) And I saw the beast [Asshur], and the kings of the earth, and their armies, gathered together to make war against him that sat on the horse [Christ], and against his army [his wife]. (20) And **the beast was taken**, and with him the **false prophet** that wrought miracles before him, with which he deceived them that had received the mark of the beast, and them that worshipped his image. **These both were cast alive into a lake of fire burning with brimstone**.

In Isaiah 30:31–33 we saw that Asshur the Assyrian, was indeed cast into Tophet, the place of fire ordained for him. But Isaiah 14: 15–18 also shows that he first goes to the sides of the pit. He is subject to the ridicule and questions of the leaders of other nations, which are already in Hell and are the nations of the uncircumcised. Although Asshur is dead, slain by the sword, only his body is dead. Asshur's spirit and soul (psyche) are still very much alive and aware of what is transpiring. He is alive when he enters Tophet, the lake of fire.

Revelation 17

"A scarlet coloured beast"

Revelation 17 is closely related to chapters 13 and 12 as it pertains to the beast with seven heads and ten horns. Chapter 17 adds a dimension, which is called "Mystery, Babylon The Great, The Mother Of Harlots And Abominations Of The Earth." The identity of Babylon the Great will not be discussed in this chapter, but we will look into the relationship.

The chapter starts with one of the seven angels of the seven vials, of the seven plagues. This angel states that his purpose is to show John the judgment of the great whore that sitteth on many waters. The woman is seen sitting on a beast having seven heads and ten horns.

> (1) And there came one of the seven angels which had the seven vials, and talked with me, saying unto me , Come hither; I will shew unto thee the judgment of **the great whore that sitteth**

upon many waters: (2) With whom the kings of the earth have committed fornication, and the inhabitants of the earth have been made drunk with the wine of her fornication. (3) So he carried me away in the spirit into the wilderness: and I saw a woman sit upon **a scarlet coloured beast, full of the names of blasphemy, having seven heads and ten horns**.

The whore is obviously not Satan's kingdom but is riding upon Satan's kingdom. She is not righteous or wholesome at all, she is full of her sin, which she has freely shared with the kings or kingdoms of the earth. John is amazed as the spiritual vision continues:

(4) And the woman was arrayed in purple and scarlet colour, and decked with gold and precious stones and pearls, having a golden cup in her hand full of the abominations and filthiness of her fornication: (5) And upon her forehead was a name written, **MYSTERY, BABYLON THE GREAT, THE MOTHER OF HARLOTS AND THE ABOMINATIONS OF THE EARTH**. (6) And I saw the woman drunken with the blood of the saints, and with the blood of the martyrs of Jesus: and when I saw her, I wondered with great admiration. (7) And the angel said to me, wherefore didst thou marvel? I will tell thee the mystery of the woman, and of **the beast that carrieth her, which hath the seven heads and ten horns**.

John marvels at the sight of Babylon the Great, this in spite of the antichrist conditions he sees. She is drunk with the blood of the martyrs of Jesus (Christ). John's reaction appears to surprise the angel, and the angel asks: "Wherefore didst thou marvel?" At this point, the angel informs John that he is going *tell* him more about the woman and the beast. This is a departure from the original intent of the angel, which was to *shew* thee the *judgment* of the woman. The angel continues from verse 8 thru 17 to explain the beast, only in the last verse of chapter 17 does he define the woman. He reveals that the woman is that *great city*, which reigneth over the kings of the earth. The shewing of the judgment of the great city, Babylon the Great, is found in the entire chapter of Revelation 18.

Chapter 17:8 <u>**The beast that thou sawest was, and is not; and shall ascend out of the bottomless pit, and goeth into perdition**</u>: and they that dwell on the earth shall wonder, whose names were not written in the book of life <u>**from the foundation of the world**</u>, when they behold <u>**the beast that was and is not, and yet is.**</u>

The beast exists from the foundation of the world (kosmos) which was started at Babel, with the confounding of the tongues, and has been working behind the scene until he rises in the last days from the bottomless pit (the sides of Hell) to be manifest as the ten-king alliance. The people of the world will see this development as positive, because they have no relationship with the Lord, they are not written in the book of life.

> (9) And here is the mind which hath wisdom. <u>**The seven heads are seven mountains**</u>, on which the woman sitteth. (10) <u>**And there are seven kings**</u>: five are fallen, and one is, and the other is yet to come; and when he cometh, he must continue a short space. (11) <u>**And the beast that was, and is not, even he is the eighth, and is of the seven, and goeth into perdition**</u> (12) And <u>**the ten horns which thou sawest are ten kings**</u>, which have received no kingdom as yet; but receive power as kings one hour with the beast.

The seven heads are seven kingdoms, which have existed sequentially back through time, as noted earlier in this chapter. Here we see that five of the early kingdoms are fallen, and one of them "is," which is at the time of the writing of the book of Revelation, approximately AD 90. The final, seventh kingdom is yet to come. It will be a kingdom of ten kings, which will combine into one. This final kingdom will only last a short time (space). The beast that was, and is not, he is the *eighth, not* one of the seven heads, but is *of* them. In Revelation 13 we saw that one of the seven heads received a wound that nearly killed it, but in the *time* of the beast (Assyrian), the wound will be healed, and the world will be amazed. Many people believe that the beast that was and is not, will be the one who receives the wound, but verse 11 clearly shows him as the eighth, not one of the seven.

If the beast, the Assyrian, is not the one who receives the wound and is healed, who is? One key is the fact that the Assyrian is **of** the seven. He is part of the seven heads because he is "*Assyrian.*" He is ethnically from Assyria. We saw in Isaiah 23:13 that the Assyrian founds the nation for them who are in the wilderness, who are no nation. We saw that this is to be an end time event. If the Assyrian will be the king of Assyria, then the nation of Assyria, which appears to be dead and gone today will have to be healed! The nation of Assyria suffered a wound which caused the Assyrian Diaspora 1918, but Assyria has never quite died. **THIS WILL BE A SIGN: WATCH ASSYRIA REVIVE.**

> (13) These [the ten Kings] have one mind, and shall give their power and strength unto the beast. (14) **These shall make war with the Lamb**, and the Lamb shall overcome them: for he is the Lord of lords, and King of kings: and they that are with him are called, and chosen, and faithful. (15) and he saith to me, The waters which thou sawest, where the whore sitteth, are peoples, and multitudes, and nations and tongues. (16) And **the ten horns which thou sawest upon the beast, these shall hate the whore, and shall maker her desolate and naked, and shall eat her flesh and burn her with fire**. (17) For God hath put in their hearts to fulfil his will, and to agree, and give their kingdom unto the beast, until the words of God shall be fulfilled. (18) And the woman which thou sawest is that **great city**, which **reigneth over the kings of the earth**.

The ten kings, who will arise, will unite and agree to give their power and authority to the beast for specific purposes—the first being to burn and destroy Babylon the great, the woman who is riding them. It becomes clear that the relationship between the ten kings and the woman is not harmonious. They hate her. Her destruction is best accomplished through an alliance with Asshur. Asshur has control of a formidable force, he controls the former three beasts of Daniel, the lion, bear and leopard. He also controls Persia (Iran), he overflowed Iran with the arms of a flood (Daniel 11:22).

The second purpose is to defy God and fight the establishment of Christ's kingdom, they ally with the Assyrian to do battle against the

Lord. They don't do so well. They are overcome by the Lamb (the man from Bethlehem) and his army, the called, the chosen, and the faithful. This is the same battle as seen in Isaiah 31:9:

> And he [the Assyrian] shall pass over to his strong hold for fear, and his princes shall be afraid of the ensign, saith the Lord, whose fire is in Zion, and his furnace in Jerusalem.

The battle is seen in Revelation 19:19 and Joel 2:10 and 11:

> (19) And I saw the beast, and the kings of the earth, and their armies, gathered together to make war against him that sat on the horse, the King of kings and Lord of Lords and against his army, his wife hath made herself ready.

> Joel 2:10: The earth shall quake before them; the heavens shall tremble: the sun and the moon shall be dark, and the stars shall withdraw their shining: (11) And the Lord shall utter his voice before his army: for his camp is very great: for he is strong that executed his word: for the day of the LORD is great and very terrible; and who can abide it?

This battle between the beast and his armies and the Lord and his armies has been commonly called by the name Armageddon. This title is because of its location in Israel. The final battle is situated in the area just north of Judea near the ancient city of Meggido, the place called Armageddon. The battle is also referred to as the "battle of that great day of God Almighty."

> Revelation 16:13-16: (13) And I saw **three unclean spirits like frogs come out of the mouth of the dragon, and out of the mouth of the beast, and out of the mouth of the false prophet**. (14) For **they are the spirits of devils**, working miracles, which go forth unto the kings of the earth and of the whole world, to gather them to the battle of the great day of God Almighty. (15) Behold, I come as a thief. Blessed is he that watcheth, and keepeth his garments, lest he walk naked, and

they see his shame. (16) **And he gathered them together into a place called in the Hebrew tongue Armageddon**.

It is clear from these scriptures that demons are behind the thoughts and actions of the beast (Asshur) and the false prophet. The demons are gathering all those to the slaughter who hate God and have taken the mark of the beast. Satan and his demons hate mankind and desire to see this battle. John is allowed to see these spirits, so we will know that this is not just a battle of man against God but also the work of demons. Note, the *whole* world is gathered against the Lord. This would indicate that the righteous are no longer in the world. The sheep and the goats have been separated. They are those who get the victory over the beast and have entered into the Lords kingdom.

> Revelation 15: (2) And I saw as it were a sea of glass mingled with fire: and them that had **gotten the victory over the beast**, and over his image, and over his mark, and over the number of his name, stand on the sea of glass, having the harps of God. (3) And they sing the song of Moses the servant of God, and the song of the Lamb, saying, Great and marvelous are thy works, Lord God Almighty; just and true are thy ways, thou King of saints.

The victory comes to those who serve God and can sing the song of the redeemed, the song of the Lamb. They know their Lord Jesus and will follow him. They also overcame him (Satan) by the blood of the Lamb and the word of their testimony, and they loved not their lives unto the death (Revelation 12:11). No matter what you are told, *you* can have the victory through *your* relationship and fidelity to Christ.

Those who decide to serve the beast have many trials to deal with. They will pay a great price for their rebellion.

> Revelation 14: (11) And the smoke of their torment ascendeth up for ever and ever: and they have no rest day nor night, who worship the beast and his image, and whosoever receiveth the mark of his name.

Revelation. 16: (9) And men were scorched with great heat, and blasphemed the name of God, which hath power over these plagues: and they repented not to give him glory. (10) And the fifth angel poured out his vial upon the seat of the beast; and **his kingdom was full of darkness**; and they gnawed their tongues for pain, (11) And blasphemed the God of heaven because of their pains and their sores, and **repented not of their deeds**.

What a horrible price to pay for rebellion!

The Ten Horns

The ten horns, which receive power as kings for one hour with the beast, are the **final kingdom of men** to exist before God sets up his kingdom, which will see no end. Because Asshur will take over this kingdom and use it for his purposes, I want to develop our understanding of this kingdom. We already know that these kings give their kingdom to Asshur to destroy Babylon the Great (the woman) and to fight God in the day of the Lord, we also know they are in unity in these endeavors, but at some point, Asshur destroys three of these kings. This will happen shortly after Asshur enters Jerusalem and sets himself up to be worshipped. Three of the kings probably take exception to this act, and this rebellion will be punished.

The final kingdom of ten kings can also be seen in Daniel 2. King Nebuchadnezzar had a dream about a great image, and Daniel gave him the interpretation of the dream.

(31) Thou O king, sawest, and behold **a great image**. This great image, whose brightness was excellent stood before thee; and the form thereof was terrible. (32)This image's **head was fine gold, his breast and his arms of silver, his belly and his thighs of brass, (33) His legs of iron, his feet part of iron and part of clay**. (34) Thou sawest till that a stone was cut without hands, which smote the image upon his feet that were of iron and clay, and brake them to pieces.

This was a single great image, but its parts are made of different materials. Daniel continues to interpret for the king:

> (37) Thou, o king, art a king of kings: for the God of heaven hath given thee a kingdom, power, and strength, and glory. (38) And wheresoever the children of men dwell, the beasts of the field and the fowls of the heaven hath he given into thine hand, and hath made thee ruler over them all. **Thou art this head of gold**. (39) And **after thee** shall arise another kingdom inferior to thee, and another **third** kingdom of brass, which shall bear rule over all the earth. (40) And the **fourth** kingdom shall be strong as iron: forasmuch as iron breaketh in pieces and subdueth all things: and as iron breaketh all these, shall it break in pieces and bruise. (41) And whereas thou sawest **the feet and toes, part of potters' clay and part of iron, the kingdom shall be divided**; but there shall be in it the strength of iron, forasmuch as thou sawest the iron mixed with miry clay. (42) And as the toes of the feet were part of iron, and part of clay, **so the kingdom shall be partly strong, and partly broken**. (43) And whereas thou sawest iron mixed with miry clay, **they shall mingle themselves with the seed of men but they shall not cleave one to another**, even as iron is not mixed with clay. (44) **And in the days of these kings (the ten toes) shall the God of heaven set up a kingdom**, which shall never be destroyed: and the kingdom shall not be left to other people, but it shall break in pieces and consume all these kingdoms, and it shall stand for ever.

These kingdoms, which started with Babylon, the head of gold, and continued *sequentially* until the final kingdom, which is the ten toes, fell before the Lord in the end. In the days of the ten toes, the Lord will establish his kingdom, which will last forever.

The list of these kingdoms revealed in the great image are as follows: Babylon (the head), Medes, Persians (breast and two arms), Greeks (belly), Romans (two legs of iron). The ten toes, upon which the final judgment falls, are the beasts kingdom. This list matches the list of kingdoms in Revelations 17:10, except having five kingdoms fallen, which would mean that the list starts with Egypt instead of Babylon as shown in the great image of Daniel 2.

This ten-nation confederacy will have some major problems. Five toes are from the eastern Roman Empire, and five toes are from the western Roman Empire. There has always been a cultural divide between east and west. There is a disparity between the nations in strength—all are not equal. Also the symbolism of clay and iron symbolizes different peoples that cannot mingle. They have an alliance but don't fully trust each other. They don't have the strength of full unity.

The Assyrian is ideally suited to lead such an alliance: he is western in his religious tradition and eastern in his cultural and political background. When he breaks with the Holy covenant and plots with those who forsake the Holy covenant, to attack Jerusalem, it will be difficult to hold the alliance together, thus the "tidings from the north" and the destruction of three horns. This alliance is used to deal with the ships of Chittim, which stopped the Assyrian from entering Jerusalem and causes his retreat.

Descriptive Summary of Revelation 13 and 17.

1. John sees a beast come up out of the sea with seven heads and ten horns. This beast is an extension of Daniel's chapter 7 beast. Verses 13:1, 17:3

2. Satan is shown to be the head and power of the beast. Verse 13:3

3. The people of the world worship the beast (the man). Verses 13:4 and 8

4. The beast (the man), the eighth king, is Asshur, the Assyrian. Verses 13:5–7 and 17:11.

5. A beast called the false prophet is revealed, and he assists the Asshur in his world control. Verses 13:11–17.

6. Asshur seals his followers with a mark, or his name, or the number of his name, in the right hand or their forehead. Verses, 13:16–18.

7. Assyria the nation will be revived at that time by Asshur, the eighth beast. Verses, 13:3 and 14, 17:10.

8. The ten kings will give their kingdoms and power to the Asshur for the purpose to destroy Babylon the Great and to fight the armies of God at Armageddon. Asshur and ten kings are defeated. Verses, 17:12–14.

CHAPTER FIVE

Asshur the Son of Perdition

Chapter 2 of II Thessalonians is without doubt the clearest and most concise account of the man we know as the Assyrian.

> (1) Now we beseech you, brethren, by the coming of our Lord Jesus Christ, and by our gathering together unto him, (2) That ye be not soon shaken in mind, or be troubled, neither by spirit, nor by word, nor as letter as from us, as that the day of Christ is at hand.

This account starts by a clarification of prophetic events: the coming of the Lord, or the Parousia of the Lord, and the gathering of the saints unto him. The Parousia of the Lord is the "day of the Lord" the day of his return to judge the nations; he will come *with his saints* to set up a kingdom. This is the event that we have already seen in Revelation 19, where his wife has made herself ready, and she is given white robes and set upon horses to *return with him* as his army. The gathering together unto him is a different event, where the Lord calls his bride, those who love his appearing, to be caught up to him in the clouds. They are taken by him to his father's house for the purpose of *becoming* his wife, the marriage of the Lamb. This event is promised in John 14:2–3,

> (2) In my Father's house are many mansions: if it were not so, I would have told you. **I go to prepare a place for you**. (3) And if I go and prepare a place for you, **I will come again, and**

> **receive you unto myself**; [gathering unto him] that where I
> am, there ye may be also. [in his father's house]

These two events are closely linked and both important, but
someone had been asserting to the Thessalonians that the day of Christ
was at hand or about to happen. They are told not be shaken by these
reports.

> (3) Let no man deceive you by any means: for that day shall
> not come, except there come **a falling away first**, and that **man
> of sin** be revealed, the **son of perdition**; (4) Who opposeth
> and **exhalteth himself above all that is called God**, or that
> is worshipped; **that he as God sitteth in the temple of God,
> shewing himself that he is God**. (5) Remember ye not, that,
> when I was yet with you, I told you these things? (6) And now
> ye know what withholdeth that he might be revealed in his
> time.

There will be a falling away. People will be turning their back on
the ways of God. Their values, priorities, and morals will not be from
God. The experts of that time will be smarter than God and exempt
themselves from any obligation to God or his word.

There will also be the revealing of a man. He is called "that man of
sin" and the "son of perdition." We can see that this is a single man—
"that man" "the son"—not a group of men or the trend of a nation but
literally "a man." This man will epitomize sin, willfully violating the
laws and will of God. The term "perdition" is only used a few times in
scripture and has a severe meaning. The term is first used in describing
Judas Iscariot, the betrayer of Jesus on the night of the last supper. The
term is also used to describe the beast that comes out of the bottomless
pit and goeth into perdition. The word perdition means to be destined
for Hell, or damned. We have detailed in previous chapters in this
book that the Assyrian has an appointment with Hell and that Tophet,
the place of fire, is ordained for him.

The descriptions and definitions we find in this chapter are
remarkably similar to those we see in the Book of Revelation, which
we studied in the chapter on Asshur and the beast. The book of

Thessalonians was written about forty years prior to Revelations. The doctrine about the son of perdition was firmly in place within the church prior to John's revelation on Patmos. The Thessalonians are reminded that they had already been told these things. They must have derived the understanding from the Old Testament prophets, Isaiah, Daniel, Ezekiel, and Micah. It is possible that Paul also had an understanding of the Assyrian/Persian connection to the man of sin.

The man of sin exalts himself above *all* that is called God. He has absolutely no need for God. He desires to completely erase anything that pertains to God and put himself in that place, even to the point of evicting God out of his own temple and setting himself up a throne in the temple. We know from the abundance of scripture that this act is called the abomination of desolation. Jesus used this event as a central key to the final events at the end of the age.

In verse 6 we find the term "revealed in his time." No matter how hard we look or how diligently we study, this man will only be revealed in his time: the time that *God* has ordained, the time that God has set for the events to take place. Remember, God told Daniel that these events are for the time of the end.

> (7) For the **mystery of iniquity** doth already work: only he who now letteth will let, until he be taken out of the way. (8) And then shall **that Wicked** be revealed, whom the Lord shall consume with the spirit of his mouth, and shall destroy with the brightness of his coming:

We are told that the mystery of iniquity doth already work. This means that, as of AD 50, the operational plan of Satan and his ministers is already being implemented and carried out. Certainly, much more work and preparation has been done now, in our time. The followers of the prince of this world have persecuted Christians and Jews many times since biblical times, but they has never been able to overcome them. Satan has been allowed to tempt and harass God's people. The trials of this life are used by God to mold the character of his people and teach them his ways. It says that this will be the situation in this world until he that letteth be taken out of the way. The Spirit of God, the Holy Spirit, is working in this world to draw men to God and to convict men of sin; this Holy Spirit ministry will come to an end at some point during the end times. The iniquity that is offered to the world is that there is an alternative to serving and worshipping the Lord, this comes in the form of many false religions and false prophets, and ending in the final ultimate manifestation of the Antichrist, the man of sin and perdition. The word "Antichrist" as found in I John 2:18:

> (18) Little children, it is the last time: and as ye have heard that antichrist shall come, even now are there many antichrists; whereby we know that it is the last time.

The word "Antichrist" used in this scripture is a compound word: anti and Christ. The word "anti" means "instead of, or in place of," and thus is an alternative to "Christos" the Messiah. We know that Asshur is the man that opposes Christ and his kingdom, and he is really more than just an alternative to Christ—he seeks to destroy him and his people and replace Christ as God. Asshur does not believe that God can stop him; he believes that his will is stronger than the will of God.

Asshur is given yet another title, "that Wicked," which the Lord shall consume with the spirit of his mouth. We know from John 1, that Jesus is the Logos of God, the Word, and that he created the world, all that there is. Nothing has been made that he did not make. He created everything by speaking them into being; this is the positive use of the spirit of his mouth. Asshur will be confronted by the Lord's anger and the wrath of his mouth; we see in Revelations 19:15 that the Lord uses his mouth as a sword to smite the nations (the beast and his confederates).

(15) And **out of his mouth goeth a sharp sword, that with it he should smite the nations**:…

Christ also consumes Asshur and his followers with the brightness of his coming, Parousia. We see an account of the reaction to this event in Revelation 6:15–17:

> (15) And the kings of the earth, and the great men, and the rich

men, and the chief captains, and the mighty men, and every bondman, and every free man, hid themselves in the dens and in the rock of the mountains; (16) And said to the mountains and rocks, Fall on us, and hide us from the face of him that sitteth on the throne, and from **the wrath of the Lamb**: (17) **For the great day of his wrath is come**; and who shall be able to stand?

Following after Asshur may be an alternative to Christ, but in the end, it isn't the place you will want to be. Note: if you do not belong to Christ, and are not a part of his bride, you will find your position somewhere with the people in the descriptions of verse 15 above.

II Thessalonians chapter two continues:

> (9) Even **him, whose coming is after the working of Satan** with all power and signs and lying wonders, (10) And with all deceivableness of unrighteousness in **them that perish**; because they receive not the love of the truth, that they might be saved. (11) And for this cause God shall send them **strong delusion**, that they should believe a lie: (12) That they all might be damned **who believe not the truth**, but had pleasure in unrighteousness.

Again, we see that Asshur's power is not his own but is from Satan. He receives his ability to deceive and do signs and wonders from Satan, Asshur himself is deceived by Satan into believing that he himself is the source of the power. This strong delusion is allowed by God to continue until judgment comes. The delusion starts because the people have refused to receive the love of the truth. When a person's attitude towards the truth or the gospel is one of rejection, all they can receive is the lie. They are disposed to receive lies because they reject the truth. They will accept Asshur's claims because he is the alternative to the truth, he is "Antichrist." His codes of conduct will be embraced because they will be far looser than the Lord's and the consequences for sin removed, they will have pleasure in these new unrighteous laws, remember, Asshur seeks to change time and laws (Daniel 7:25).

The final five verses of II Thessalonians 2 are a shining contrast to the previous verses of the chapter. They highlight God's will and desire for his people, those who believe the truth.

> (13) But we are bound to give thanks always to God for you, brethren beloved of the Lord, because God hath from the beginning chosen you to **salvation through sanctification of the Spirit and belief of the truth**: (14) Wherefore he called you by our gospel, to the obtaining of the glory of our Lord Jesus Christ. (15) Therefore, brethren, stand fast, and hold the traditions which ye have been taught, whether by word, or our epistle. (16) **Now our Lord Jesus Christ himself, and God, even our father, which hath loved us, and given us everlasting consolation and good hope through grace**, (17) **Comfort your hearts**, and establish you in every good word and work.

The Thessalonians, to whom this account was written, are referred to as beloved of God. How did they become so loved? There is a twofold explanation given. First, there is a sanctification of the spirit. Sanctification is a process of separation: separation from the things of this world, unto the things of God. This sanctification is a spiritual operation. It cannot begin until a person is born of the spirit. Secondly, "belief in the truth": when someone yields to God's ways and will, and professes their belief in God's word, through faith, their salvation is assured.

They were also called by the gospel of the apostles of Jesus unto the truths of who Jesus is and what he has done for all men who call upon him. There is salvation in no other name. There is a tremendous consolation, or comfort, in God for those who trust his grace

This world system is on a collision course with God, the nations will gather to fight the Lord; it is essential that you choose to follow God in order to avoid their fate.

CHAPTER SIX

Asshur
One Man's Story

Based on all the scriptural information revealed about the man simply called Asshur the Assyrian, the information we know about the Assyrian people and the current world situation, I want to figuratively paint a picture of him and his affect on the end of this age.

We must remember or at least acknowledge that he is indeed a man, and as a man he has a family. He has at a minimum a father and mother, and probably brothers and sisters, and, as with most ethnic communities, a host of direct and indirect family members: aunts, uncles, cousins, etc. As is the case with all of us, we are molded by our family during the early years of our lives. Asshur is no different. Only thirty or forty years before his birth, his family and indeed the entire Assyrian community in Iran had been subjected to what is called "the Genocide."

During the first world war, the Turks and Kurds attempted to remove all trace of the Assyrian people from lake Urmia area of northern Iran. These acts of barbarism were not limited to Iran, they took place also within the Assyrian homeland areas within Iraq. The Assyrians had few options at the time. They could flee, usually to Russia, they could hide, or be killed. There was also the option of renouncing their Christianity and converting to Islam. The evidence implies that few Assyrians chose the converting option. It seems they preferred to die as Christians than to live as Moslems.

Two thirds of the Assyrian nation perished during the Genocide, and only about fifteen-thousand Assyrians were left alive in Iran after

WWI. It is likely that Asshur's family was a part of that remnant and would be carrying the humiliation and wounds of that event. During WWI, the Assyrians had two allies, but the relationship was much different between the two. First, the Russians, who were portrayed by war annals and other personal Assyrian documents as humane, friendly, and compassionate, while the British, the second, were seen as aloof, haughty, and exploitive. I'm sure that there are exceptions in both cases, but the general feeling (or bias) would be a part of Asshur's early life.

There were other peoples in the Lake Urmia area during WWI which had to flee, such as the Armenians and Greeks, The difference was that they had a homeland to flee to, which would open to them and allow them to recover. The Assyrian nation's institutions, which had been maintained since ancient times, did not survive the Genocide. The people were dispersed throughout the region and eventually around the world. The Assyrian Diaspora had begun:, the wound to the head, which appears to be unto death.

But the Assyrian people are not gone, and they, like the Jews before them, have a desire to reestablish their nation in their God given homeland. As a young man, Asshur will share this desire, and this will become a large part of his motivation and drive. Before the dreams of restoration can be realized, the Assyrians must deal with the true situation, that of just surviving. The Assyrian people are very intelligent and resilient; they are slowly building a foundation from which to move forward. They have the Lord to lean upon, and though the world may not recognize them, their God has never forsaken them. No matter where they are in the world, what far land they have landed in, he hears their cries and their prayers. This young man, Asshur will some day be used, according to Isaiah 23, to found the revived nation of Assyria.

It is amazing that, by and large, the Assyrian people have not become bitter and vengeful toward the peoples that have treated them so horribly. They have refused to return the hatred and avenge themselves. They simply want to go home and live in peace. This is without a doubt a tribute to their Christian testimony and their genuine love for Christ and his ways.

Before Asshur can become a leader in the Iranian government, he must first become successful professionally within the Assyrian community of Iran. He will be looked up to as someone who can represent them well. He will share their desire and hopes for the future. He will be well spoken and an able communicator. He will at some point become not just the Assyrian leader of the Assyrian community in Iran but also lead all those of the Diaspora as well. He must be able to unite the entire Assyrian nation. He will need to convince an otherwise indifferent world community that the Assyrian cause is just and in the best interest of the world at large and that a revived Assyria has value to Iraq and will add stability to entire region. According to scripture, he will be up to the task.

Upon the establishment of the Assyrian province, in whatever form it will take, Asshur will need to govern and lead it into respectability and prosperity. There are some that maintain that the Nineveh Plain has a vast undeveloped oil resource and that it belongs to the Assyrian people. If this is true, it may explain why Asshur is so successful in founding the nation. Isaiah 23:13 states that he set up the towers (defenses) and raised up palaces—these activities require organization and money. We also know that Asshur will also be liberal to his people with the prosperity that comes to the nation. Some, or even most, leaders exploit their people as a resource for wealth, not as the beneficiaries. Asshur will be very popular among Assyrians for this benevolent policy. Asshur and his people have been among the poorest peoples in the world for a long time—why shouldn't they enjoy the benefits of their new prosperity? This prosperity will also encourage the Assyrians in Diaspora to return to the Nineveh Plains. There is a world of educated, talented, and motivated Assyrians just waiting for and dreaming of the day they can go home and build their nation.

The skill and success displayed by Asshur and his people will not go unnoticed. The other Iraqi provinces and neighboring nations will look with envy at the amazing recovery happening before their eyes. Asshur's prestige will grow very rapidly, and he will be respected for his abilities. His influence will begin to grow outside Assyria and Iraq, and he will be sought for counsel and advise. Asshur is called in Daniel the "little horn" that speaks great things.

This author believes that the fall of Saddam Hussein's government in Iraq is at least the first step in a process to make a way for the new Assyrian province, but it will likely require more changes to actually bring it to pass. In Isaiah 17:1 we are told that at some point in the future Damascus will be destroyed. It will be disappear as a city; it shall be a ruinous heap. Also Ammon (Jordan) will be destroyed by fire and become a desolate heap. This is found in Jeremiah 49:1 and 2 and in verse 35 to include judgment upon Elam (modern Iran). The judgment starts by stating that Iran's bow will be broken and the chief of their might. The Lord will cripple Iran, and with their military broken, they will no longer be a military threat to Israel.

The fall of Damascus (Syria), Ammon (Jordan), and Elam (Iran) will without a doubt break the back of militant Islam. Iran is to a large extent orchestrating the Islamic jihad on the western world and Israel. Asshur will take advantage of this lack of strength in Iran and move into Iran with the arms of a flood, but it will not be a battle: "He shall come in peaceably, and obtain the kingdom (Iran) by flatteries." The public spin for his actions will be something like this: "For the sake of peace and stability in the region, I have taken control."

With the demise of Syria, Jordan, and Iran, There will be a significant power vacuum in the Middle East. It is likely that the world will be so shaken by these developments that there will rise a ten-nation confederacy, an alliance of nations to attempt to insure stability. This new alliance will transcend cultures, geographic location, and religious differences. This new group will be made up of five nations from Europe and five from the Asia and the Middle East. Alliances between the east and west have always been shaky at best, and usually short lived.

While the need for a unity alliance is the reason for bringing this confederacy into being, it will have a weakness because of the different cultures and religions (partly of iron and partly clay), and it will need a strong leader to maintain stability and give direction. Asshur is the little horn, the eleventh king, which will rise up from within the ten horns. He is the little horn that is more stout that the others and has a mouth speaking great things. Asshur is the perfect leader for this new alliance. He is Iranian by nationality (Eastern) and Western by religion (Assyrian), and he will appeal to everyone involved.

The military and economic strength of this ten-nation group is very attractive to Asshur. We will then see the part of his character he becomes known for—anger. His early motivation was the national restoration of the Assyrian people, but now we see his anger. Just below the surface of his persona boils a pot of simmering rage. Asshur sees an opportunity to get even with the many nations, which brutalized, broke promises to, or refused to recognize the Assyrian people. We know from Isaiah 10 that God gives Asshur a charge (order) to deal with Israel and her corruption, he was to be God's rod of discipline, but he has his own plans to destroy nations, and not a few. The problem with vengeance is that it clouds the judgment and feeds upon itself. Soon anyone who gets in his way will be dealt with severely.

Asshur's move into Iran will be his first real step outside Assyria, but soon after he would be challenged by Egypt. Egypt is the last real military power in the region and will see no reason to submit to the little horn with the big mouth. There quickly develops a need for diplomatic talks to take place between Asshur and the leader of Egypt. Daniel 11 states that both Asshur and the leader of Egypt will speak lies at one table, and that Asshur will strike Egypt militarily and destroy her. This attack is provoked by Egypt because of the closure of the Suez Canal to Israel (Ezekiel 29:9 and 10). Israel has had a peace treaty with Egypt since 1975, and an article of that treaty allows Israel undiscriminate use of the Suez Canal. Failure to allow Israel use of the canal is an act of war.

Asshur has made a seven-year security agreement with Israel to insure that none of Israel's enemies would ever attack her again. The destruction of Syria and Jordan by Israel happened because they attacked Israel, God said: "Israel, thou art my battle ax and weapons of war: for with thee will I break in pieces the nations" (Jeremiah 51:20). Egypt may feel compelled to respond by closing the Canal, and thus giving Asshur the excuse he needs to attack

> Daniel 11:25: And he [Asshur] shall stir up his power and his courage against the king of the south [Egypt] with a great army; and the king of the south shall be stirred up to battle with a very great and mighty army; but he [Egypt]) shall not stand:...

Asshur will return to Assyria with the spoils of war—great riches— and his heart shall be against the holy covenant. After the destruction of Egypt, something happens to turn Asshur against God and against the holy covenant God has with his people, both Jew and Christian.

There is no specific information given in scripture to allow us to know what happened. It is possible that he resents having to support Israel when his true sentiments would be anti-Semitic. In order to make sure that this never happens again he will desire to break his covenant with Israel by attacking and taking her. This is what he attempts to do. He shall return and come toward the south (holy land).

But it shall not be as like the last time, for the ships of Chittim will come against him. Therefore he will be grieved and return to Assyria. Chittim is a general term, which applies to the Isles of the sea, and is not specific. Asshur commands a formidable army and for a naval force to stop his land advance it would have to be a task force that possesses naval air power. Both Britain and Russia are under the domination of the ten-nation alliance, which is under the control of Asshur. The ships of Chittim will not be from them. We find that China will at a future time come with a land force into the Middle East but not with her navy. The only naval power capable of this kind of deterrent is the United States. America has been a friend of Israel many times in the past and appears to step in to help her one more time.

It is not in the scope of this book to explore in depth the subject of America in prophecy, but some basic understanding of the subject needs to be injected at this point. In Micah 5 we find an account of a military campaign between Israel and Assyria. This battle takes place at the time that Messiah returns to Israel after a long absence. The Messiah will bring peace to Israel when the Assyrian comes into Israel; the Messiah is the man from Bethlehem who is from old to everlasting. A group of fifteen Israeli leaders will be assembled to lead an attack into Assyria, which includes the land of Nimrod. The land of Nimrod is Babylon, the southern part of Mesopotamia, the plain of Shinar. Assyria will not be confined to a small province in northern Iraq but will control all of modern Iraq. The entire area will be wasted by the Israeli attack (Micah 5–6). It is this author's opinion that the entire land of Assyria, including Nimrod's land, the south, will be restored and become the work of God's hand (Isaiah 19:15). This Israeli attack will be at the end of Daniel's seventieth week, the end of Jacobs's trouble, and the beginning of Christ's millennial kingdom.

The biblical accounts of the destruction of Babylon, as found in Jeremiah 50 and 51; Isaiah 13 and 47; Revelation 17 and 18; and

Ezekiel 17 all paint a completely different scenario for the destruction of Babylon. First, the accounts all describe Babylon as the *greatest* nation in the world, not as a southern province of Assyria. Babylon is called the "hammer of the whole earth." (Jeremiah 50:23). She is the greatest global military power and stands alone in that position. Her demise will require an assembly of nations to accomplish.

> Jeremiah 50:9: For, lo, I [the Lord] will raise and cause to come against Babylon an assembly of great nations from the north country: and they shall set themselves in array against her; from thence she shall be taken:....
> Jeremiah 50:41 Behold a people shall come from the north, and a great nation, and **many kings** shall be raised up from the coasts of the earth.

This attack against Babylon has never taken place in history, and the scriptural context is prophetic to the end times. The accounts tell us who some of the attacking nations are.

> Jeremiah 51:27and 28 Set ye up a standard in the land, blow the trumpet among the nations, prepare the nations against her [Babylon], call together against her the kingdoms of Ararat, Minni, and Ashchenaz.... (28) Prepare against her the nations with the Kings of the Medes....

These nations in modern terms are Russia (Ashchenaz), Iran (Minni and the Medes), and Turkey (Ararat). The result of this attack is described in Jeremiah:

> (50:13) Because of the wrath Lord it [Babylon] shall **not be inhabited**, but it shall be **wholly desolate**;...
> (50:39) ...and it (Babylon) shall be **no more inhabited for ever**, neither shall it be dwelt in from generation to generation.
> (51:29) And **the land** shall tremble and sorrow: for every purpose of the Lord shall be performed against Babylon, to make **the land** of Babylon a **desolation without an inhabitant**.
> (51:37) And Babylon shall become heaps, a dwelling place

for dragons, an astonishment, and an hissing, **without an inhabitant**.

(51:43) Her **cities** are a desolation, a **dry land** and a wilderness, **a land** wherein no man dwelleth…

This destruction is forever and complete. It includes all the land of Babylon and all her cities. It is the end of Babylon's identity as a nation. The description of end-time Babylon, which is also known as the "Daughter of Babylon" (Isaiah 47:1, Jeremiah 50:42, 51:33) is very complete and revealing:

1. The greatest military power in the world. Jeremiah 50:23

2. She will be great at the same time as Israel's restoration to their land (1948). Isaiah 14:1; Jeremiah 50:4–7, 51:19 and 20; Ezekiel 17:22–24.

3. Her national symbol is an Eagle. Ezekiel 17:7.

4. She is the greatest economic nation in the world. Revelations. 18:11 and 17.

5. She is the world's largest consumer nation. Revelations. 18:11.

6. She is nation of mingled people. People from many nations woven together into one. Jeremiah 50:37.

7. She was a golden cup in the Lord's hand. A nation used to bless the rest of the nations of the world. Jeremiah. 51:7; Isaiah 47:1.

8. She becomes perverted. She trusts in her own wisdom and knowledge. Revelations. 18:2; Isaiah 47:1 and 10; Jeremiah. 51:7.

9. She is a nation where the Jewish people will immigrate, prosper, and grow wealthy, from which they return to the land of Israel.

10. She becomes full of the occult, witchcraft, and sorceries. Revelation 18:23; Isaiah 47:9, 12, 13.

11. She is proud and considers herself a queen. She is called the "Lady of Kingdoms." Revelation 18:7; Isaiah 47:1, 5, 7.

If you compare Iraq to the descriptions given above, especially given the Jewish issues, you can not reconcile modern Iraq with the Daughter of Babylon.

If Iraq is not the daughter of Babylon—who is? In Revelation 11:8 we find a passage, which will help answer this question. This verse refers to a time near the end of the age, just prior to the Lord's return. God has ordained two witnesses to preach in the city of Jerusalem at that time. When these witnesses have finished their testimony, they are overcome and killed:

> (11:8) And their dead bodies shall lie in the street of that great city, which spiritually is called Sodom and Egypt, where also our Lord was crucified.

The great city is none other than Jerusalem! And because of the spiritual condition of the city, it will be called Sodom and Egypt. It is not a matter of geographical location, but rather a spiritual condition. Jerusalem will in that day acquire the spirit of Sodom and Egypt. With this in mind, we can look for a nation that acquires the spirit of Babylon, which matches the description of the Daughter of Babylon, not the geographic location of the land of Nimrod. The Daughter of Babylon is an allegorical name for an end-time nation, which did not exist at the time of the writing of the prophecies.

By applying the descriptions to the time of Israel's restoration, because the Jews come out of Babylon to go back to their land, we find that the only nation that fits the description is America. America doesn't just fit some or most of the descriptions, it fits all of them perfectly. The odds of this being just a coincidence are considerable. This author calculated (using compound probability) the odds of any one nation fitting the description to be in excess of 10 billion to 1.

So, there are two end-time Babylon's in scripture. One is Iraq under the control of the Assyrian and called the Land of Nimrod. It is attacked from the south by Israelis and wasted. The second is America, called the Daughter of Babylon and is attacked from the north by an assembly of great nations including Iran and Russia. It is completely destroyed never to be inhabited.

If this subject of America in prophecy is of interest to the reader, this author has written a book called *America the Daughter of Babylon* which deals with the subject in detail.

The ships of Chittim turned Asshur back from going into Israel, and we are told he has indignation against the Holy Covenant and will conspire with those who have forsaken the Holy Covenant. Israel represents the Holy Covenant and so do the ships of Chittim. By referring to the Holy Covenant, scripture is talking about Christians and Jews. There will be nations who have had the testimony and tradition of Christianity but have forsaken the covenant of God and backslidden into Apostasy. These nations will hate Israel and America and what they represent: the Holy Covenant. The ships of Chittim must be dealt with and removed from the situation. An assembly of great nations attacking from the north will do this, and America's navy will be neutralized.

America has long been the deterrent against Russia's desire to destroy Israel, and with America gone, Russia feels free to attack Israel. Little do they suspect that this is a trap set by the Lord himself. They will attack despite the Assyrian's covenant with Israel. Russia, the king of the north, will push at him (the Assyrian). This attack is not unexpected by Israel, and they, with God's help will destroy the Russian army and air force on the mountains of northern Israel.

> (Ezekiel 39:1, 2, 4, 6): (1) Therefore, thou son of man, prophesy against Gog, and say, Thus saith the Lord GOD; Behold, I am Against thee, O Gog, the chief prince of Meshech and Tubal: (2) And I will turn thee back, and leave but a sixth part of thee, and will cause thee to come up from the north parts, and will bring thee upon the mountains of Israel. (4) Thou shalt fall upon the mountains of Israel, thou, and all thy bands, and the people that is with thee: I will give thee onto the ravenous birds of every sort, and to the beasts of the field to be devoured. (6) And I will send a fire on Magog, and among them that dwell carelessly in the isles: and they shall know that I am the LORD.

Only one sixth of the Russian army or forces are left alive; five sixth of them die on the mountains of northern Israel,. God also sends fire upon Magog, the Russian homeland. The fire upon Magog has an association with fire falling upon those who live carelessly in the Isles. Who are those living carelessly in the Isles? The ships of Chittim are from the Isles of the sea, and if as this author asserts, the daughter of Babylon and Chittim are both allegorical names for America, then both Russia and America are burned with fire. In Jeremiah 51:13 we find that the Daughter of Babylon "dwelleth upon many waters" and in Isaiah 47:8 she "dwelleth carelessly."

The fire falling on Russia and America may be a nuclear exchange from which both will suffer horribly. The demise of the Daughter of Babylon and her destruction by fire is documented extensively in scripture, but the burning of Magog is only seen in Ezekiel 39:8.

At this point in Asshur's life, he is the leader of Assyria, which includes all of Iraq. He is in control of Iran (Persia) and he has seen the destruction of Damascus (Syria), Ammon (Jordan), Egypt, Magog (Russia), and the Daughter of Babylon (America). Asshur has also become the leader of a group of ten nations, five from Europe and five from the Middle East. He used the armies of this alliance to attack and destroy both Egypt and America.

Asshur is now in the position to move into Israel and Jerusalem and vent his indignation against the Holy Covenant and the Jews. He will approach Jerusalem from the West Bank (Judea). At this point, those living in Jerusalem and the surrounding area, which do not trust the Assyrian and, more importantly, are obedient to the scripture, will flee to the mountains and wilderness. There is only one area open to their flight: Moab and Edom. Both Moab and Edom have escaped Asshur's advance.

> Daniel 11:41: He [Asshur] shall enter also into the glorious land, and many countries shall be overthrown: **but these shall escape out of his hand, even Edom, and Moab...**

It is probable that Asshur ignores the area because it has no strategic importance and virtually no population. He will ignore the remnant of Judeans existing in this wilderness for a period of time because he has much to do.

There is at this time no illusion that Asshur is a man of peace or that he can be trusted, he has broken his agreement with Israel. This is the mid point of Daniel's seventieth week, and Asshur will rule from Jerusalem for the next three and one half years. He will now set himself up to be worshipped in the Jewish temple. This is his attempt to prove that the God of Israel and Christians has no say or power in the affairs of man or the world. This is the time that he departs completely from his fathers and their beliefs and the remnants of the Assyrian church. The success that he as a leader has enjoyed he believes comes from his own innate abilities and powers. He will now start rewriting laws and times, he will establish his will as law, and his values will govern the world. The false prophet will be his assistant in convincing the world that he is worthy of worship, and he institutes the economic control of the mark of his name. His name can now be called "Antichrist" because he is presented as the alternative to Christ and truly becomes the Beast. He is totally self-centered and demon possessed. We see this in Revelation 16:13:

> (13) And I saw three **unclean spirits** like frogs come out of the mouth of the dragon, and **out of the mouth of the beast** [Asshur] and out of the mouth of the false prophet. (14)For they are **the spirits of devils**, working miracles, which go forth unto the kings of the earth and the whole world, to gather them to the battle of that great day of God Almighty.

Not everyone in the world is ready to capitulate to Asshur and his plans for their lives. He will receive tidings or news from the east. This would be the kings of Asia, which have remained neutral up to this time. We are told that the Euphrates River is dried up that the way of the kings of the east might be prepared (Revelation. 16:12). The kings (plural) will come as a 200-million man army (Revelation 9:16). Asshur goes out with fury to do away with them and destroys them, This can not be a conventional battle, and he must use weapons of mass destruction. The kings of the east could represent the nations of China, India, and Japan, but may be more inclusive with nations like Korea and Indonesia. They are no longer a threat to Asshur or his false prophet. However, Asshur also receives news from the north: the only source left in the north is Asshur's own five-nation alliance of apostate nations. We are told that Asshur will destroy three of these nations. We are not told any specifics, but if they don't like his policies or get on board with his agenda, Asshur has no room for compromise.

> Daniel 7: (8) I considered the horns, and behold, there came up among them another little horn, before whom there were **three of the first horns plucked up by the roots**: and, behold, in this horn were eyes like the eyes of man, and a mouth speaking great things.
> (20) And of the ten horns that were in his head, and of the other which came up, and **before whom three fell**; even of the horn that had eyes, and a month that spake great things, whose look was more stout than his fellows.

All ten of these kings (horns) were in unity at the time of the destruction of Babylon the great, which was just a short time before he receives tiding from the north.

> Revelation 17:16–17: And the ten horns which thou sawest upon the beast, these shall hate the whore, [Babylon the great] and shall make her desolate and naked, and shall eat her flesh, and burn her with fire. (17) For God hath put in their hearts to fulfil his will, **and to agree, and give their kingdom unto the beast (Asshur)** until the words of God be fulfilled.

This author believes that the tiding from the north is dissention from three of Asshur's original five northern allies. He destroys them because he no longer needs them.

Asshur will now turn his attention to the Judeans hiding in the wilderness, in the place prepared for them by God. We are told in Revelation 12:14 that a place has been prepared by God for this remnant to hide for three and one half years, or forty-two months. There is a location in Edom today, which is ideal for a refuge. It is called Petra, an abandoned ancient fortress city on the east side of the Dead Sea. The modern Israelis know of this site and love to visit it when possible. When the Messiah returns to deliver his people, he will go first to Edom and then to Jerusalem.

Isaiah 63: (1) Who is this that **cometh from Edom**, with dyed garments from Bozrah? this that is glorious in his apparel, travelling in the greatness of his strength? I that speak in righteousness, mighty to save. (2) Wherefore art thou red in thine apparel, and thy garments like him that treadeth in the winefat? (3) I have **trodden the winepress** alone; and of the people there was none with me: and **I will tread them in my anger, and trample them in my fury**; and their **blood shall be sprinkled upon my garments**, and I will stain all my raiment. (4) For the day of my vengeance is in my heart, and the year of my redeemed is come.

This event is also seen in Revelation 19:11–15

(11) And I saw heaven opened, and behold a white horse; and he that sat upon him was called Faithful and True, and in righteousness he doth judge and make war. (12) His eyes were as a flame of fire, and on his head were many crowns; and he had a name written, that no man knew, but himself. (13) And **he was clothed with a vesture dipped in blood**: and his name is called the Word of God. (14) And the armies which are in heaven followed him upon white horses, clothed in fine linen, white and clean. (15) And out of his mouth goeth a sharp sword, that with it he should smite the nations: and he shall rule them with a rod of iron: and **he treadeth the winepress of the fierceness and wrath of Almighty God**.

What an incredible sight this will be, when the Lord returns to deliver his remnant from the wilderness, to judge the nations, and to set up his kingdom, which includes judging Asshur. Asshur sees the ensign of the Lord coming his way and runs in fear. He will run to a stronghold, a place where he will have maximum protection and security. We don't know for sure where it is, but it will likely be close to Jerusalem so he can reach it quickly. It is in this stronghold that he is killed by the sword (or knife). He will be assassinated by someone in that bunker, someone who will not be a soldier or a fighter, but is an ordinary man. He is in the bunker, so he is considered important or valuable. His ability to get close to Asshur means he is probably a counselor or consultant, certainly high ranking and trusted. Thus, will Asshur leave this life. He leaves the nations of the world devastated and in turmoil. At the news of his death, the world will sing and rejoice. The oppressor is gone. Asshur has left this world but has only gone into next. The nations of the uncircumcised residing in Hell are raised up to greet his arrival. They belittle him and mock him, but his stay in the pit is only temporary. His final destination is Tophet, the place of fire, the lake of fire. His destiny as the "son of perdition" is eternal torment. God had said that he would punish Asshur after he had performed his complete work in Zion, and he has. God will now set about cleansing the temple and setting up his kingdom.

> Daniel 7:26–28: But the judgment shall sit, and they shall take away his (Asshur's) dominion, to consume and to destroy it unto the end. (27) And the kingdom and dominion, and the greatness of the kingdom under the whole heaven, shall be given to the people of the saints of the most High, whose kingdom is an everlasting kingdom, and all dominions shall serve and obey him. (28) **Hitherto is the end of the matter**…

Final Comments

It is good to remember that the scriptural accounts and scenarios are not just possibilities for future events but rather are the actual event given to those who are willing to read and study. The biggest challenge to the student of scripture is to look at all the references on a given subject and to compare scripture with scripture. The exposition you have just read is my best attempt to explain how I have come to understand these scriptures and to arrange them in order. I've been waiting many years for the proper time to write this exposition, and it is my conviction that if I wait any longer, some of the events may become history not prophecy. More information and developments will undoubtedly come to light, as we come closer to the fulfillment of these events, requiring modifications and adjustments to the accounts.

It is also necessary to accept the message and situations as they are revealed in scripture and not allow our own personal preferences or ideas to taint them. God is righteous, and his judgments are always proper. We tend to judge without the full understanding and with only finite information—God can always be trusted to do right.

God sees the Assyrian people in terms of the final disposition of the nation: that is, the work of his hands. It is important for us to allow God to deal with them, as well as Israel, and for us to see beyond God's process of sanctification and to see the glorious age to come. God chastens those he loves.

Dear reader, God loves you also, and you have value to God. He desires to do a work of sanctification in your life. You can't control the direction this world will take and the decisions that others will make, but you can choose your path and your direction. Seek God, and he will be found. Yield to his gospel and Holy Spirit, and he will direct your path. God has sent his son to redeem you to himself through his sacrifice on the cross. Jesus died for you. Accept him and he will accept you: no one is excluded.

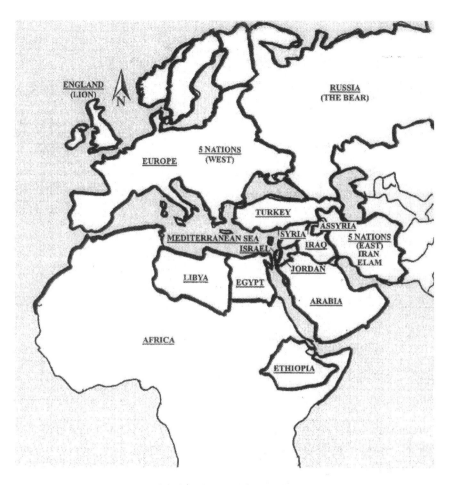

MEDITERRANIAN
AREA

MAP-1

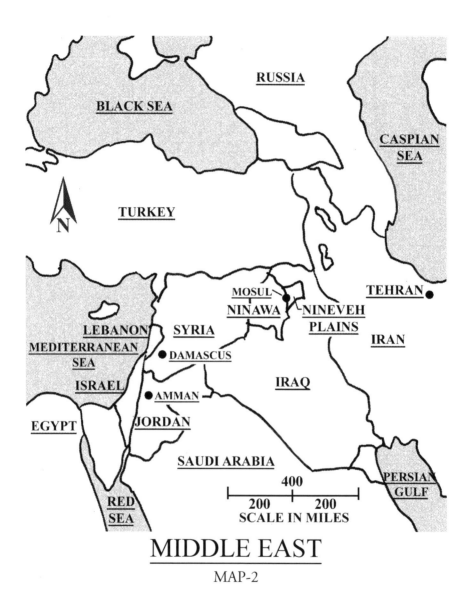

MIDDLE EAST

MAP-2

IRAQ
MAP-3

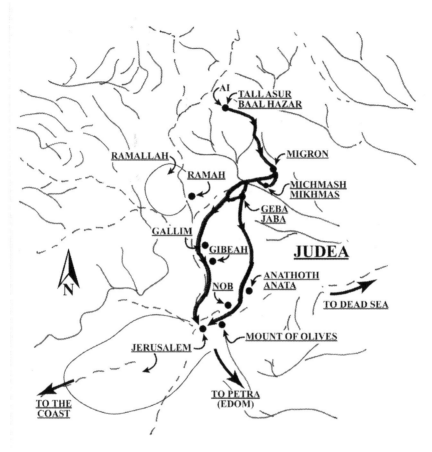

JUDEA and JERUSALEM

MAP-4

GENERAL INDEX

Abomination of Desolation: 8,33,38,69
Armageddon: 36,37,39,60,61,65
Assyrian Churches: 2,84

Bear: 41,60

Dead Sea: 84
Diaspora: 2,5,6,8,20,33,59,74,75
Dry places: 20

Eagle: 80
Euphrates River: 37,84

False Prophet: 55,56,61,64,84,85

Gehenna: 26
Genocide: 73,74
Great Tribulation: 3

Hinnom: 26

Islam: 2,76

Leopard: 41,60
Lion: 41,60

Meshech: 23
Messianic: 3
Millennium: 3,7
Mother of Harlots: 56,57

Nineveh Plains: 2,20

Parousia: 67,70
Petra: 84

Small people: 31,32
Son of Perdition: 68,87
Soviet Union: 36

Terrorist: 23
Tophet: 25-28,44,56,87
Tsunami: 18
Tubal: 23

West Bank: 15,16,83

INDEX OF NAMES

Gentiles: 6-8
Greeks: 63,74

Hebrews: 5:15
Holy Spirit: 70,88

Iscariot: 68
Israel: 78,79,81.86

Jesus: 7,57,61,67,69,70,72,88
Jews: 1,6,8,16,21,30,33,35,69,78,80,82-84
Judeans: 85

Kurds: 73

Lucifer: 1,24,34,39,48,53

Magog: 83
Medes: 2,46,51,62,79
Messiah: 6-8,11,13,70,78,86
Micah: 5,8,11
Moslem: 33,74

Nazis: 35
Nebuchadnezzer: 17,62
Nimrod: 3,34,52,78,79,81
Noah: 1

Osirus: 1

Pentecostal: 2
Persian: 49,60,63

Roman: 63,64
Russian: 74,83

Sargon I: 1
Saddam Hussein: 2,76
Satan: 24,34,48,49,52,55,57,61,64,69,71
Shem: 1
Sumerians: 2
Syriac: 2

Turks: 73

INDEX OF PLACES

Iran: 23,29,34,60,73,75,76,79,82
Iraq: 1,2,34,73,75,76,78,80,81
Israel: 6-9,11-13,15,16,21,25,28,32,34-36,60,76-78,81-84,88

Jaba: 14
Japan: 37,84
Jerusalem: 7, 8, 10, 12-16, 19, 25-28, 33, 34, 36-38, 43, 53, 60, 64, 81, 86, 87
Jordan: 2,23,76,77,83
Judea: 7,8,12-14, 16,19,35,37,43,60,83,84

Korea: 85

Lebanon: 19,23

Madmenah: 15
Media: 29
Meggido: 60
Mesopotamia: 1,2,78
Michmash: 14
Mikhmas: 14
Moab: 37,83

Nineveh: 1,2,20,75
Nob: 15

Palestine: 19
Patmos: 69
Persia: 29,30,32,34,38,46,51,60

Ramah: 15
Ramallah: 15
Rehoboth: 1
Rome: 51
Russia: 36,37,73,78,79,82

Shinar: 1,78

Sidon/Zidon: 16-21
Sodom: 81
Syria: 2,76,77,83

Turkey: 79
Tyre/Tyrus: 16-21

United States: 33,78
Urmia: 73,74

Zion: 12,13,15,25,28,35,60,87

SCRIPTURE INDEX

Revelations:
Chapter 9: p.37,84
Chapter 12: p.52,61,85
Chapter 13: p.51,52,64
Chapter 14: p.61
Chapter 15: p.61
Chapter 16: p.37,60,62,84
Chapter 17: p.56,64,85
Chapter 19: p.56,60,70,84,86